Pastoral Care: A Thematic Approach

Pastoral Care: A Thematic Approach

by

DONALD CAPPS

THE WESTMINSTER PRESS
Philadelphia

BOOK DESIGN BY DOROTHY ALDEN SMITH

First edition

Published by The Westminster Press®
Philadelphia, Pennsylvania

PRINTED IN THE UNITED STATES OF AMERICA

1 2 3 4 5 6 7 8 9

Library of Congress Cataloging in Publication Data

Capps, Donald.
Pastoral care.

Includes bibliographical references.
1. Pastoral psychology. 2. Pastoral theology.
I. Title.
BV4012.C317   253   78-15093
ISBN 0-664-24222-7

TO KAREN AND JOHN

Contents

Preface

PASTORAL CARE is most effective when it is based on a strong theoretical foundation. A minister cannot be optimally effective in pastoral care without a clear understanding of what is done and why it is done. Unfortunately, since the middle 1960's, the theoretical foundations of pastoral care have been deficient. Pastoral psychology and pastoral theology, the traditional foundations of pastoral care, have lost much of their earlier vitality. While they were strong in the 1950's and early 1960's, they are not very strong today.

Attempts since the middle 1960's to establish pastoral care on alternative theoretical foundations have not been particularly successful. The task before us today therefore is to revitalize pastoral psychology and pastoral theology so that they can again provide the necessary theoretical bases for the effective practice of pastoral care.

This book is largely, though not exclusively, an exercise in pastoral psychology. To provide a sound foundation for pastoral care, it employs a psychological perspective that has been used extensively in both study and practice but has never been formulated into a consistent theory. I call this perspective the "thematic approach to the study of human personality." This perspective claims Erik H. Erikson as its leading representative today. Through his emphasis on the role that psychosocial themes play in the formation of human personality, Erikson has done much to give this psychological perspective an identity of its own. Before Erikson came on the scene, the thematic approach to the study of the human personality had its various proponents, but few psychologists and educators believed that the study of the human personality could be organized around the thematic analysis of personality. Through his life cycle theory, Erikson demonstrated that a thematic approach to personality theory could provide a comprehensive understanding of the human personality.

Seminary professors and students have long recognized the value of Erikson's views. His works have been read extensively in seminary courses, and numerous articles have been written on Erikson's life cycle theory and its implications for pastoral care. But what has not yet been attempted is to formulate his thematic perspective into a comprehensive theory. His views have been applied to a variety of practical problems and issues in ministry, but they have not been organized and developed in such a manner as to provide a theoretical foundation for pastoral care. The purpose of this book is to demonstrate how the thematic approach to the study of the human personality, especially as represented in the work of Erik Erikson, can be developed into such a theoretical foundation.

I hasten to point out, however, that there are other ways to carry out a theoretical task than by formulating a tightly knit argument. Erikson referred to his book *Childhood and Society* as a "conceptual itinerary." I have conceived this book in a similar way as a conceptual itinerary, not a systematically formulated theoretical statement. I wanted there to be a conceptual progression in my handling of the focal interests of pastoral care (personality change, local church dynamics, pastoral counseling, ministry in crisis situations), but I also wanted this itinerary to be flexible and open-ended. The earlier robust venturesomeness of pastoral care has too often been replaced with the neatly packaged tour. My concern for open-endedness also accounts for the absence of a concluding theoretical statement. As Erikson observes in the concluding chapter of *Childhood and Society*, "I must concede that whatever message has not been conveyed by my description and discourse has but a slim chance of being furthered by a formal conclusion. I have nothing to offer except a way of looking at things."

I have also relied heavily on case materials in carrying out this theoretical task. *Childhood and Society* demonstrates that case materials may embody as well as illustrate theories and concepts. As a reader who likes to get to a book's basic substance as efficiently as possible, I empathize with a reader's inclination to skip over case materials. At the same time, I recognize that this inclination is not unlike the pastor's disposition to avoid parishioners because they get in the way of effective ministry, or the teacher's desire to avoid students because they frustrate the goals of education. In the course of writing this book, my desire to develop a clear and precise theory of pastoral care was continually intruded on by the case materials included in this book. I felt like the hero of Bunyan's *Pilgrim's Progress*, who simply wanted to get to the Promised Land as expeditiously as possible but kept meeting all those people along the way. But, like Bunyan's hero, I also began to realize that the road to the Promised Land is arduous and the Celestial City more distant than one had originally assumed. So I not only began to welcome the company these case materials offered, I also allowed them to help determine my itinerary.

I would like to thank Rev. Daniel Davila for his contribution to this book and Dean Joe R. Jones of The Graduate Seminary at Phillips University for encouraging this project.

D.C.

1
The Thematic Approach to Personal Change

A FRIEND relates to you an incident about a man you both know. He concludes his account with the comment: "I knew Jim would do that. Knowing him, he could not have reacted in any other way." Another friend comes to you puzzled and perhaps a bit angry. He tells you what a mutual friend has just done and comments, "I was really surprised. It was so out of character for him."

What makes people act in certain characteristic ways? Why can we be counted on to respond in certain ways when confronted with certain situations? And why do we find it so hard to change these characteristic patterns of behavior once they are firmly established?

Psychologists have discussed this issue and offered various interpretations. Some have explained it in motivational terms. They have said that we act the way we do because we have certain motivations that are permanent. We have sexual needs, needs for power and influence, needs to belong, and needs to overcome felt deficiencies. Others have suggested that we act in characteristic ways because we each have a set of basic traits. We may be naturally generous rather than niggardly, self-assured rather than self-effacing, friendly rather than hostile, gregarious rather than withdrawn. Others have noted that we act in characteristic ways because we have developed a particular set of attitudes and habits. We habitually follow other people's advice rather than make our own decisions. We habitually play it safe rather than take risks. We are habitually cautious rather than impulsive in our decisions.

Still other psychologists have said that we act in characteristic ways because we have certain goals for ourselves. These may be extrinsic goals, such as the desire to succeed in our profession. Or they may be intrinsic goals, such as self-fulfillment, the desire for personal integration and wholeness or for ultimate peace and quiescence. Then there are psychologists who place particular emphasis on the role of emotions and moods in influencing us to act in certain ways. They suggest that a person may be counted on to respond to virtually any difficult situation with strong emotion. Some people are subject to rather extreme mood swings from high elation to deep depression while others are characteristically calm and controlled.

The list of psychological explanations could go on and on. There is undoubtedly merit in each of these proposals. No doubt the reason we develop characteristic ways of acting is a complex matter and cannot be reduced to a single explanation. In any case, it has been an important question for psychologists in general and personality theorists in particular. In my judgement, it also has particular importance for pastoral care.

In caring for another person, the pastor is sometimes called upon to support this person's characteristic way of acting in most situations: "You have always done it this way and I see no reason why you should change just because this has happened." At other times, the pastor is called upon to question a person's characteristic way of acting in order that a more desirable response to the present situation might become possible: "I know this is how you usually handle situations like this, but I suspect that you yourself sense that it isn't working out."

This book is primarily about the latter pastoral role because it is the role that pastors tend to find most difficult. It is usually easier—though I would not claim that any pastoral role is easy these days—to confirm parishioners in their customary patterns of behavior. To question parishioners' characteristic ways of responding to situations in life is usually more difficult. The pastor does not want to offend a parishioner, to undercut the only real stability the parishioner's life may have. To invite the parishioner to take new courses of action may be risky and threatening. Yet I am persuaded that the need to break out of these characteristic patterns is not merely one that the pastor imposes on parishioners. It is a need that many parishioners already recognize within themselves but find difficult to act upon without encouragement or blessing. They are restrained from acting on this need, and pastors are restrained from helping them to act on it.

This book, then, is mainly concerned with the pastor's role in helping individuals change their characteristic ways of responding to life's situations. In the later chapters I will discuss how the pastor's counseling ministry may assist parishioners toward this objective, how personal crises intensify the need to break out of characteristic patterns of behavior, and how this need is present in groups as well as individuals. First, however, I want to address this issue in more general terms. What does it mean to say that individuals are locked into customary ways of relating to their world? What is implied in the argument that they have a need to break out of these characteristic patterns?

The thematic approach to the study of the human personality has special value because it recognizes the complexity of these patterns. It takes seriously their adaptational quality, and it understands that these patterns are not merely the effect of past habit but rather continue to have a strong intentional thrust. Furthermore, the thematic approach to personality does not say that personal change and transformation can occur only if these characteristic patterns are totally dismantled. On the contrary, it contends that these patterns must be the basis on which such transformations occur. In practical terms, this means that the characteristic pattern cannot simply be ignored or trampled upon as pastor and parishioner work toward change and transformation. The customary pattern itself holds the key to these transformations.

However, before we can discuss the role these patterns play in personal growth we need to clarify the concept of "theme" as the thematic approach to personality employs it.

The Concept of Theme

The term "theme" is commonly employed in the arts. In music, it refers to the principal melody of a composition. In literature, it refers to the central idea of the work. Its use in the psychological sciences is not as familiar to us. However, it has been used by some psychologists to identify the continuity and direction inherent in characteristic patterns of personality. Thus, themes refer to the continuity and direction within the basic structure of the personality. But since the term "theme" is not very descriptive by itself, the psychologists we will be discussing here have used a variety of more descriptive terms: personality themes, life themes, unity themes, psychosocial themes, perennial themes. It is not my intention to make fine distinctions between these various descriptive terms. I shall feel free to use each of them wherever appropriate. The important point is that the psychologists who have recommended these various descriptive terms reflect considerable unanimity on the concept of theme itself.

To get at the concept of theme, let us think for a moment about the way that literary works, especially biographies, autobiographies, and novels, describe the unfolding life of the major protagonist. The writer's task is to show how the personality of the principal character in the story develops over a period of time. Does this character grow in personal stature and quality? Or does he cease to develop, and perhaps even turn in upon himself? These are the sorts of questions the biographer, autobiographer, or novelist are expected to address. In fact, one of the most serious criticisms that can be leveled at a literary work of this nature is that the author has failed to show character or personality development when (in the case of biography or autobiography) there was such development or when (in the case of the novel) the author's purposes clearly demand it.

How does the author show this development? One of the most effective ways is to identify the *principal themes* in the subject's personality, and then to show how these themes undergo change as the life unfolds. If the protagonist is mainly affected by power and political influence, what do we learn about this individual's personality through the vicissitudes of his pursuit and exercise of power? Does his quest for power undergo significant changes during his lifetime? If so, do these changes reflect a personality that is growing, or do they reflect a personality whose development has atrophied?

The good author knows he or she cannot do justice to the whole complexity of the subject's personality by focusing on the unfolding of a *single* theme. A minor character in the story may be developed in terms of a single theme. In such a case the reader knows that the author is not attempting to capture the complete personality of this minor character but is in effect giving us a caricature or stereotype. In the case of the major character in the story, however, development of the personality in terms of a single theme is rarely adequate. In fact, the way to make this character interesting from both a dramatic and a psychological standpoint is to show how two or more themes struggle for dominance within the personality. The subject's exercise of power may be offset or even contradicted by a strong mystical interest, as in Dag Hammarskjöld's autobiographical *Markings*. It is the thematic complexity, two seemingly incompatible themes within a single personality structure, that makes this subject interesting. This thematic complexity also makes the major actor in the story truer to life, beset with the same conflicts and contradictions that beset us all.

Besides using themes and thematic patterns to illuminate personality development, the biographer, autobiographer, and novelist pay considerable attention to the *social context* in which the personality takes shape. These authors share the conviction that the development of the personality does not take place in a social vacuum. On the contrary, development takes place in a social context of considerable complexity. It involves numerous interactions not only with other persons but also with a variety of social institutions. Even though an autobiography or biography is the story of one person's life, it would be quite odd if the author failed to introduce others who were influential in the development of this life. We are puzzled when an autobiographer fails to say anything at all about his or her parents, family, and work associates. As John Donne said, no man is an island. The literary artist recognizes this. And because it is not possible to mention all of the protagonist's social interactions, certain ones, especially revealing of how the subject characteristically related to his social world, are selected. Did the subject typically relate to other people in terms of what was wanted from them? Were they treated with condescension or mistrust? The author understands that the principal themes in the personality of his subject are developed and revised in interaction with the social environment.

What does this brief excursion into literature tell us about the psychological concept of theme? First, the psychological perspective discussed in this book uses the concept of theme to describe the basic personal interests or intentions that direct an individual's life. By means of the notion of theme, these psychologists are able to chart the development of the personality over a period of time. Some themes persist without much variation, others undergo significant change, and still others appear to atrophy and die. Using themes in this way the psychologist is able to conceptualize these processes and describe how they function.

Second, these psychologists stress the fact that the thematic structures of the individual personality are not simple but complex. If an individual personality reflects a dominant theme, the pattern will nonetheless also reflect a variety of subordinate themes that can significantly influence the way the dominant theme will express itself in concrete actions.

Third, themes express interactions between the individual and his social environment. They express interactions of power, love, hostility, affection, trust, manipulation, and so on. Thus, themes are not merely "personal" in the sense of being private and subjective. They are also psychosocial, involving interactions with another individual, groups of individuals, and social institutions. Furthermore, themes tend to express characteristic patterns of psychosocial interaction. Psychosocial themes do not apply to casual interactions, e.g., buying a gallon of milk at the neighborhood grocery store. One may buy milk at a particular store regularly, and may therefore claim that this action is characteristic ("Every Tuesday, Thursday, and Saturday I go into Roy's Supermarket to buy a gallon of milk"). Rather, the interactions that invite thematic analysis are those that capture the basic intentionalities of the personality. For example, why do one's relationships with work associates always begin with high expectation and soon degenerate into hostility and backbiting? This is the sort of social interaction that the thematic approach to the study of personality seeks to address.

Major Representatives of the Thematic Approach to Personality

While Erik Erikson is the most widely known representative of the thematic approach to the study of personality, there are other significant figures. We will have occasion to talk about four psychologists, including Erikson, who are representatives of this tradition. The following is a brief thumbnail sketch of these four and their contribution to the thematic approach.

Henry Murray. The psychologist who first gave thematic analysis a central place in the study of personality is Henry Murray. Among his many accomplishments during his involvement in the Harvard Psychological Clinic, Murray is perhaps best known today for his development of the Thematic Apperception Test. This is a commonly used projective instrument designed to assist in the thematic analysis of personality. This test requires subjects to tell stories about themselves in response to a set of pictures. Because each picture includes two or more persons, the stories involve interaction between them. These stories are then subjected to a thematic analysis designed to identify the subject's major personality themes. Murray has extended this thematic approach to personality to the study of novels, myths, and other literary products.

Robert W. White. Also associated with the Harvard Psychological Clinic, White is best known for his emphasis on the role of competence motivation in the development of the young child. He holds the view that children are not merely motivated by security needs but also have an inherent need to achieve competence and skill. This view is part of his larger concern with the more complex and flexible aspects of personal development. He emphasizes the fact that personality is a constantly evolving system subject to continuous change. By using the Thematic Apperception Test to chart the changes in personality over time, White is able to conceptualize personality changes in thematic terms.

Erik H. Erikson. Erikson was already an established child analyst when, among his various relationships in Boston, he became associated with the Harvard Psychological Clinic in 1933. His original contribution to the thematic approach to personality was to extend the Thematic Apperception Test to the study of children through their play constructions. He would ask children to create a scene from the toys placed at their disposal, and then would proceed to analyze the scene in terms of its basic personality themes. Erikson later extended this emphasis in his studies of rituals of American Indians, and of the lives of Martin Luther and Mahatma Gandhi. In these latter studies, he analyzed key events in the lives of Luther and Gandhi in much the same way that he analyzed the children's scenes. He is best known for his life cycle theory, which views personality growth and development in terms of psychosocial themes.

Robert Jay Lifton. A psychiatrist whose work has been greatly influenced by Erikson, Lifton is probably best known for his work on the relation between personality development and sociocultural change. In his studies of the survivors of the bombing of Hiroshima in World War II, of American veterans of the Vietnam war, and his observations on contemporary youth in various cultures, Lifton has shown that psychosocial themes reflect the negative as well as positive role played by the social environment in personality development. In his major essay, "Protean Man," Lifton suggests that the personality of contemporary man is less oriented around continuity and direction and more oriented around discontinuity and change.

Having identified the major representatives of the thematic approach to the study of the human personality, I would now like to discuss how the concept of theme has developed beyond the basic essentials outlined above. Since Murray and Erikson have given most attention to developing the concept itself, I will describe Murray's distinction between simple, complex, and unity themes, and then Erikson's notion of psychosocial themes as developed in his life cycle theory.

Murray's Contribution to the Concept of Theme

To Henry Murray, a theme expresses an individual's interaction with a segment of his environment.[1] A theme identifies the personal interest that prompts an individual to interact in a particular way, and how a segment of the environment influences him to make him act in this manner. The phrase "man bites dog" that sometimes appears in newspaper headlines illustrates this interactional view of themes. In this case, the man is the individual, the dog is the segment of his environment, and biting is the form of interaction that takes place between the man and the dog. In Murray's terminology, "man bites dog" expresses the *simple theme* of this interaction.

To describe the interest of the individual and the influence of the environment in its situational complexity, we need to go beyond the simple theme to a description of the *complex theme*. If we were to read the newspaper article and not merely the headline, we might discover that the man's unusual behavior was motivated by the dog's previous act of biting the man. We might also discover that the man was a mail carrier and that the dog had allegedly been nipping at his heels for many days prior to today's incident. We might also learn the outcome of this incident. The mail carrier promises his supervisor that the incident will not happen again and the dog's owner promises to keep the animal under stricter surveillance. As for the dog, he seems unaffected by the incident, showing no signs of permanent physical damage and indicating no remorse. The complex theme goes beyond the formal features of the interaction between man and dog. It specifies persons and roles, the personal interests and environmental influences involved in the interaction, and the various forms this theme has taken in the past and may take in the future.

In addition to the simple and complex theme, Murray identifies the *unity theme.* In his view, the human personality is not motivated simply by the whims of the moment or by the instigating influence of the social environment. Rather, the individual develops enduring needs for certain kinds of interactions with the environment. These enduring interests issue in a stable pattern of interactions that Murray calls a *unity theme.* In his view, it is possible for a person to have more than one unity theme, with such themes integrating a number of smaller interests. Two or more unity themes may operate together, either in the form of clusters or in a series, i.e., one unity theme relating to another in a discernible temporal sequence.

An example of a unity theme is expressed in the country song that includes the line, "I'm going to keep on falling in love till I get it right." In this case, the singer is not merely waiting for a segment of her environment to instigate the interaction. On the contrary, there is a strong disposition to initiate a specific type of interaction, namely, love. And, because this predisposition to "fall in love" is an enduring interest, it constitutes a unity theme. Unity themes do not reflect occasional needs but continuing interests.

This example also illustrates another of our major interests in applying thematic analysis of the personality to pastoral care. It is our concern with thematic variations and their implications for personality change. The individual who proposes to keep falling in love "till I get it right" does not anticipate that every love relationship will have the same outcome. At some point, if one is persistent enough, one will experience a variation on the theme of falling in love. Someday, it will be "right."

By continuing to fall in love, subjecting oneself to the inevitability of more failures, eventually one will succeed. And, in succeeding, there is no need to abandon interest in love itself. Rather, one will be in love to stay. Thus, the "till I get it right" represents a variation on the theme "I'm going to keep on falling in love."

In analyzing responses to the Thematic Apperception Test, (TAT), Murray and his associates were especially interested in subjects' formulations of variations on basic unity themes. Such variations are exceedingly important for personal change. They express the individual's sense of having options and not merely being consigned to an unvarying future. Thus, thematic variations reflect the possibility of significant personal change.

One of Robert White's cases in *Lives in Progress* provides an excellent illustration of this link between thematic variation and personality change. White and his co-workers identify three unity themes in Joseph Kidd's TAT stories.[2] The first centers around the longing and loneliness engendered by the loss of a loved person; generally, this loved person was an older man. The second theme is that of bitterness and hate; several of his heroes bear grudges against the world and seem to feel that everyone is against them. The third theme involves the transformation of his cruelty and greed by the sympathetic interest of an older man.

All three themes depict the hero in interaction with some segment of his environment (i.e., interpersonal interaction), and all three describe the nature of this interaction (i.e., loneliness, bitterness and hate, cruelty and greed). But only the third theme proposes a variant form of interaction. This theme envisions the transformation of cruelty and greed into more positive forms of interaction. This more positive interaction is made possible by the sympathetic interest of an older man. Thus, this theme expresses Kidd's sense of how his life can be significantly altered. In fact, it offers his solution to the problems expressed in the first and second themes (i.e., the loss of a loved person and the perception of the whole world as being against him). If the variation on the third theme can be brought to pass, Kidd will find such a loved person and will no longer perceive that the whole world is against him. Hence, the third theme is crucial in terms of personality change because it alone envisions a positive variation on the major unity themes of his life.

On the other hand, given the negative form of this basic theme (i.e., stories in which the older man does not appear and the hero carries out acts of cruelty and greed), Kidd is indicating that this positive outcome is by no means assured or inevitable. Personality change in this case depends on the sympathetic response of an older man. It depends, in part at least, on a responsive social environment.

The major features of Murray's development of the concept of theme can be summarized as follows:

1. *Themes reflect interaction between persons and their environments.* As Murray uses the term, theme refers to the interaction of personal interests and environmental influences. While interaction with one's environment includes the natural world, themes basically capture the interaction of individuals and their social environments. Interactions characteristically are person-to-person, though they may also involve interaction with social institutions and ideas.

2. *Unity themes reflect the enduring interests of the individual.* They do not reflect casual thoughts and feelings. Rather, they reflect the more enduring interests of the individual. Such themes are not merely reactive to environmental influences but reflect relatively permanent intentionalities of the personality.

3. *Unity themes reflect complex patterns of interaction.* Single themes coalesce to form more enduring and complex themes. These more permanent and complex themes, known as unity themes, may in turn unite to form thematic patterns. Typical patterns include: *(a)* a cluster of themes that include a dominant unity theme with various subordinate themes; *(b)* a dialectical pattern of two or more unity themes of similar intensity and duration; and *(c)* a series of themes, with one unity theme relating to another in a discernible temporal sequence.

4. *Unity themes reflect intended or actual personality change.* Variations on the unity theme or thematic pattern reflect actual or intended changes in personality. Thus, personality change can be expressed in terms of variations on unity themes. In some cases, the theme expresses a change that is positive in terms of personality growth. In other cases, it reflects a deterioration of some aspect of the personality. In still other cases, an originally clear and unambiguous theme becomes diffuse and shapeless, indicating that the personality change involves instability or temporary impairment.

Erikson's Contribution to the Concept of Theme

Erikson's understanding of themes is best reflected in his life cycle theory.[3] This theory conceives the development of the personality in eight stages, beginning with infancy and culminating in old age. Each stage involves a major psychosocial crisis, which Erikson describes in thematic terms. In the diagram, on p. 27, Column A lists the eight psychosocial themes from "Trust vs. Mistrust" to "Integrity vs. Despair." These themes are the basis of our interest in Erikson's contribution to the concept of theme.

The first point to be made about Erikson's eight psychosocial themes is that each reflects interactions of the individual and the social environment. Column B indicates the persons and groups that are most involved in shaping an individual's experience of the related theme in Column A. Column C indicates the elements of the social world that give this theme social value. Column D formulates the dynamic aspect of the interaction between individual and social environment generally reflected in this theme. By reading across the chart, we can see that the maternal person is most involved in shaping an individual's experience of trust vs. mistrust, that the society's concern with the cosmic dimension of human experience is most responsible for according the theme of trust vs. mistrust social value, and that the dynamic form of interaction between individual and society reflected in this theme is that of giving and receiving. By reading down the chart, we can see that the relationship between the individual and the social environment becomes increasingly complex. Or, as Erikson puts it, the radius of significant relations is an ever-widening one:

Personality can be said to develop according to steps predetermined in the human organism's readiness to be driven toward, to be aware of, and to interact with, a widening social radius. . . .[4]

Thus, the development of the personality begins with interaction with the mother (stage 1), proceeds to interactions involving both parents (stage 2), then to interactions with the family group (stage 3), neighborhood (stage 4), peer groups and outgroups (stage 5), partnerships (stage 6), parenthood and professional relationships (stage 7), and identification with humankind (stage 8). Erikson says that this developmental process is configurational, not unilinear, in form. This means a continuing expansion of one's social world from its center in the mother-infant relationship to its eventual encompassing of mankind in general. Thus, the interactions of the earlier themes continue to play a significant role in the later development of the personality.

Second, Erikson's emphasis on the continuing influence of earlier themes in later stages enables him to note the enduring nature of these themes. As Paul W. Pruyser points out, the themes ought not be thought of as limited to specific age levels:

Their listing in charts and diagrams of developmental progression superficially suggests that they are as specific to certain age levels as, say, the acquisition of secondary sexual characteristics in puberty. Nothing is farther from the truth. These words stand for *perennial themes* that are relevant from the cradle to the grave, but their meanings and prominence and combinations vary in highly individual ways.[5]

Erikson's eight stages are therefore not merely a series of interpersonal crises that one encounters and then puts behind as one proceeds to the next stage. A theme may predominate at a given stage in life, but it is relevant from infancy to old age.

ERIKSON'S EIGHT PSYCHOSOCIAL THEMES

	A Psychosocial Crises	B Radius of Significant Relations	C Related Elements of Social Order	D Psychosocial Modalities
I	Trust vs. Mistrust	Maternal person	Cosmic order	To get To give in return
II	Autonomy vs. Shame, Doubt	Parental persons	"Law and order"	To hold (on) To let (go)
III	Initiative vs. Guilt	Basic family	Ideal prototypes	To make (= going after) To "make like" (= playing)
IV	Industry vs. Inferiority	"Neighborhood," School	Technological elements	To make things (= completing) To make things together
V	Identity and Repudiation vs. Identity Diffusion	Peer Groups and Outgroups; Models of leadership	Ideological perspectives	To be oneself (or not to be) To share being oneself
VI	Intimacy and Solidarity vs. Isolation	Partners in friend- ship, sex, competi- tion, cooperation	Patterns of cooperation and competition	To lose and find oneself in another
VII	Generativity vs. Self-Absorption	Divided labor and shared household	Currents of education and tradition	To make be To take care of
VIII	Integrity vs. Despair	"Mankind" "My Kind"	Wisdom	To be, through having been To face not being

To identify the thematic structure of an individual personality, we cannot simply take an individual's chronological age and read down the chart until we arrive at the corresponding stage in the life cycle. Because the themes are perennial, identifying the characteristic pattern of a given personality involves assessing the relative prominence accorded the various themes without undue regard to the chronological age of the individual.

Because all eight themes are relevant from the cradle to the grave, the themes function in the personality both in a retrospective and a prospective manner. Erikson's interpreters point out that, if the psychosocial themes are in some sense sequential, this is not an invariant sequence. They cite Erikson's own suggestion that the "identity vs. identity diffusion" theme, typically confronted in critical proportions in middle to late adolescence, often involves a recapitulation of the themes encountered in early childhood. One "reworks" these earlier themes into new configurations of meaning and thereby uses past experience to shape one's identity. This is clear evidence that Erikson does not view the themes in an invariant sequence.

Variance in sequence is also seen in anticipation of crises not yet experienced in their full force. Again, the "identity vs. identity diffusion" theme is instructive, for in confronting this theme in critical proportions in middle to late adolescence, the individual is already rehearsing the themes that he will experience in their fullest impact during adulthood. It would be impossible to deal adequately with problems of identity without anticipating issues of intimacy, generativity, and integrity. Thus, while the themes are not unrelated to age and the various chronological stages of life, they are also not limited to specific age levels. If there are periods in which a theme is likely to be critical to one's personality development, the themes nonetheless transcend chronology as such and take on a perennial quality, both in a retrospective and a prospective manner.

Third, Erikson's themes are dialectical. This means that each theme reflects conflicting tendencies in one's interactions with the social environment: "trust vs. mistrust," "autonomy vs. shame and self-doubt," and so on. This dialectical view of themes is crucial to Erikson's understanding of the development and growth of the personality. In his view, personal growth is reflected in an individual's capacity to interact with his social world in such manner that the two "poles" of the theme are not allowed to disintegrate into mere contradiction but to become creatively integrated into a unique personal style. Erikson cautions against assuming that the two "sides" of the psychosocial theme are merely positive and negative poles, and that the individual's task is to accentuate the positive and eliminate the negative. On the contrary, the task is to integrate the two dimensions of the theme into a unique configuration that is true to one's development as an individual. To be sure, positive growth is dependent on a preponderance of trust over mistrust, autonomy over shame and self-doubt, initiative over guilt, and so on. But if the "positive" dimension were to completely obliterate the "negative," an individual would be poorly adapted to the task of living in the real world. Mistrust, shame, self-doubt, and guilt have a place in one's interaction with the social environment.

The major features of Erikson's development of the concept of theme can be summarized as follows:

1. *Themes are psychosocial.* Themes reflect the individual's interaction with his social environment. Personality development is understood as the capacity to interact with the environment in an increasingly complex pattern of interrelationships. At the same time, the interrelationships of the earlier stages continue to exert considerable, perhaps even disproportionate, influence on the personality as it responds to the demands of this increasingly complex pattern of interrelations.

2. *Themes are perennial.* While a theme is likely to have critical importance for the individual at specified chronological stages of development, it may have special importance either before or subsequent to the stage in which it becomes critical for most individuals. The practical effect of the perennial quality of themes is that one's personality may be strongly oriented around a certain theme, and this theme may have unusual

influence on one's appropriation of other themes. In effect, a particular psychosocial theme may function in a given personality as what Murray called a unity theme.

3. *Themes are dialectical.* Murray differentiated complex from simple themes. Erikson went further and attempted to identify the nature of the complexity. He concluded that themes reflect a dynamic tension in one's relationship with the social environment. This tension is never completely overcome, but it can be dealt with creatively. One can work through this tension in dialectical fashion and thereby express the theme in a variation that is uniquely one's own. If this is not done, the elements that are in dynamic tension will eventually disintegrate into mere contradiction.

Personal Change in the Pastoral Context

These formulations of the concept of theme by Murray and Erikson enable us to explore further the issue of personal change. They provide two ways of conceptualizing personal change. Through his emphasis on unity themes and their variations, Murray captures the individual's need to break out of certain customary patterns of interacting with his social environment by securing a variation in existing thematic patterns. In similar fashion, Erikson recognizes that themes may be "reworked" in order to effect more creative integrations than were achieved at an earlier developmental stage. This indicates how an individual can transform his thematic pattern while not relinquishing the basic themes altogether. In addition, by showing that individuals can anticipate themes, Erikson recognizes that future themes may have a modulating effect on current interactions.

Four Unity Themes

Because these proposals by Murray and Erikson are highly conceptual in nature, we need to make them more concrete. Since we will be using Erikson's psychosocial themes extensively throughout this book, I will give greater attention here to Murray's emphasis on unity themes and their variations. More specifically, I want to identify four unity themes that are especially common among religious people. While I would not claim that these themes are peculiar to the types of individuals that are found in churches today, I would contend that readers of this book will be able to identify members of their own congregations who reflect one or another of these basic themes. Readers may also find themselves mirrored in one or more of these unity themes.

My procedure here will be to describe these four themes and then to indicate what a variation on each theme might involve.[6] Following this, I want to illustrate how a thematic analysis of an individual in terms of one of these themes might be developed. This illustration will suggest ways in which the pastor can identify the characteristic patterns by which an individual interacts with the social environment and, by identifying these patterns, discern ways in which they can be modified.

1. *The theme of resignation.* This theme is reflected in individuals who are characteristically torn between two conflicting courses of action. Such individuals seem to possess two "opposing wills" that cannot be easily reconciled. But they recognize that this opposition must eventually be resolved. This can be accomplished by relinquishing one of the opposing courses of action and committing oneself singlemindedly to the other. It can also be accomplished by recentering one's basic interests, which will require relinquishing desirable features of both "opposing wills." Whichever way the conflict is resolved, the resolution itself is frequently experienced as a special divine intervention, an act of God. There is often a disclosure, revelation, or special illumination that confirms the course this individual has chosen. This theme is called "resignation" because it influences the individual to resign himself to one or another course of action. As a relatively permanent theme, it means that the individual views the whole course of life as one in which many interests and desires were renounced because they

were seen to conflict with other interests and desires that were chosen.

2. *The theme of suffering.* A second theme is exhibited in individuals who describe themselves as the victims of an unhealthy or hostile environment. When hurt or reproached by other people, such individuals typically believe that others act in such a hostile manner because of jealousy or envy. On the other hand, these individuals acknowledge that their own actions are sometimes motivated by self-pride. They conclude that God or other supernatural powers (e.g., Satan) are using the blandishments, slander, and treachery of other people to break their pride. In this way, they perceive their sufferings as meant for their own spiritual good. Through these sufferings and persecutions, as painful as they may be, one is being prepared for a higher purpose.

However, from time to time, these individuals also feel that the sufferings to which they are subject, whatever their ultimate purpose, are too severe. The punishment far exceeds what is necessary to dissuade them from their customary habits of blindness, obstinacy, and sin. When suffering is severe or prolonged, there may be a tendency to express misgivings concerning God's control over human affairs. Or, if God is acknowledged to be very much in control, there is an expression of doubt concerning God's benevolence. As a result, these individuals sometimes express impatience with God: What is the meaning of these sufferings? Are my sufferings essential to God's master plan? Are your blandishments simply vindictive? Could God, if he chose, put a stop to the pain that I am having to endure? In short, this theme is referred to as "suffering" because it captures a tendency of some individuals to view their lives as one set of sufferings after another. When this theme is dominant, it influences an individual to see meaning in his sufferings, and to gain an appreciation of his personal strengths as well as limitations from these sufferings.

3. *The theme of belonging.* This third theme is exhibited in individuals whose interests revolve around their relationship to a group. This group may be a religious sect or church, a particu-

lar ethnic complex within a pluralistic society, or even a nation. For these individuals, there is a direct and intimate relationship between their own interests as individuals and the purposes of the community with which they identify. Their own sense of personal fulfillment is tied up in the future of the group. If this group declines or dies out, they experience this as tantamount to their own personal death. When it flourishes, they experience this as personally confirming. Thus, their strongest personal interests and intentions are directed toward the group of which they are part.

This theme is called "belonging" because it reflects an individual's reliance on a group for the realization of his or her own deepest personal aspirations, and for support in times of personal suffering and moral uncertainty.

4. *The theme of integration.* This fourth theme is found in those individuals for whom harmony, order, and the absence of internal conflict have a particularly strong appeal. Such individuals are especially sensitive to the contradictions and contrarieties of human existence. They feel strongly impelled to overcome or transcend these contradictions in their personal lives and professional activities. Their attempts to transcend these contradictions and achieve personal wholeness, however, are usually only partially or temporarily successful. Achievement of inner harmony or personal integration is a rare and fleeting experience. While temporary experiences of this integration have special religious meaning, these experiences are also frustrating because they do not last.

This theme is both like and unlike the theme of resignation. Both themes reflect personal conflict and a longing for respite from this sense of being pulled apart. But the "resignation" theme involves resolving the conflict by relinquishing one course of action in favor of the other or, perhaps more rarely, by submitting to the process of renouncing both sets of interests in favor of other interests. The "integration" theme does not result in resolution. It maintains the conflict indefinitely because renunciation of one set of interests in favor of another would mean the loss of one important dimension of the self.

It therefore conceives personal development as a perennial tension that will never be overcome. This does not mean, however, that such individuals relinquish the desire for personal integration. They continue to long for it, and this longing gives positive stimulus to their life and work. They console themselves with the thought that, while integration is elusive, the desire for it gives vitality to their lives and creativity to their work. In short, this theme is called "integration" because it reflects a life that is strongly influenced by the desire to overcome inner contradictions. The realization of this integration, no matter how elusive it seems, is the basic intentional thrust of this personality structure.

Variations on the Four Unity Themes

This concludes our summary of four unity themes found among religious people. We turn next to the task of identifying typical variations on these themes. This is the real crux of the matter. For, while each of these themes has its positive features, it is not difficult to see that in the form in which they have been described, they can have negative effects on an individual's personal growth and development. Should any one of these themes become an individual's characteristic pattern of relating to his social world, we can anticipate that at some period in life one will strongly desire some variation on this basic theme. One may not want to relinquish this theme entirely and may indeed be unable to do so because it shapes one's whole personality. But if one is able to entertain the possibility of a variation on this theme, this variation can have a significant effect on one's subsequent personal growth. Each theme, in its own unique way, is open to variation. None of these themes is so rigid or inflexible as to disallow any variation. For example:

1. *The theme of resignation.* The individuals for whom this is a major unity theme tend to view possible courses of action as polarities. They see life in dichotomous, either-or terms. To them, resignation means being forced to decide between one

interest and another. One possible variation on this theme is suggested by Erikson's emphasis on the reworking of themes encountered earlier in life. When themes are reworked later in the light of new experiences and the passage of time, it is possible to reexperience the earlier decision in a new way. While the decision itself is in the past and in that sense irrevocable, one can reclaim elements of the course of action that was originally repudiated in favor of the opposing course. The young man who is torn between a career in law vs. the ministry and chooses the ministry, may later rework this decision and discover that he can employ in his ministry some of the intentions that law had previously symbolized for him. While this could take the form of an interest in legal aspects of the ministry, it could be something more subtle than this. For example, he may be especially sensitive to parishioners' concern for established precedents in the development of the church's programs. The individual for whom resignation is a dominant theme often regrets the past because it is strewn with abandoned hopes and aspirations. One variation on this theme, therefore, is to encourage the reclamation of the past.

2. *The theme of suffering.* Personal suffering is a fundamental aspect of this theme. It may not be possible or even desirable to attempt to eliminate the suffering itself (whether perceived or actual). But a possible variation on this theme may involve challenging the explanations an individual offers to account for his suffering. For example, the individual who believes his suffering is caused by the jealousy and envy of other people may be encouraged to consider alternative understandings of their motivations. He may simply be a scapegoat because others cannot direct their aggression against the persons or groups that are a genuine threat to them. Or one may come to a more satisfactory understanding of God's role in human suffering. The individual who believes that all his sufferings are the will of God may develop the capacity to differentiate between those sufferings that are meaningful in an ultimate sense and those that are not. If this were accomplished through Bible study (e.g., The Book of Job), it would be a case in which

Bible study performed the function of pastoral care. Variation on the theme of suffering involves gaining a more complex understanding of the reasons why one is suffering.

3. *The theme of belonging.* The individual for whom this is a dominant theme places particular emphasis on relationship to a group. It may not be desirable even if possible to attempt to eliminate this person's orientation around a particular group. But there are times when such an individual experiences the need for variations in this general theme of belonging. The person who has had predominantly negative experiences in group relations may find a subgroup within the larger group in which positive experiences become the norm. Another person for whom the group has become a personal burden may be encouraged to temporarily withdraw or disengage from some of the group's activities. While it is customary for church people to stress the positive effects of increased engagement, less is said about the positive value of disengagement. Another possible variation may involve gaining insight into one's tendency to expect the group to provide the personal identity that one must, to some extent, develop for oneself.

4. *The theme of integration.* The individual for whom this is a major theme seeks to transcend the contradictions in his life and to achieve personal harmony. This desire for personal integration is hardly to be disparaged. However, the elusiveness of the goal can be frustrating. While its elusiveness can stimulate vitality and creativity, it can also have a debilitating effect when the goal of integration takes precedence over all other interests. One possible varation on this theme, therefore, is the redirection of some of one's concern for personal integration toward outward-directed forms of integration: "He who loses his life for my sake will find it." Another variation is reflected in Erikson's life cycle theory. While the life cycle does not culminate in a complete integration of the individual personality, Erikson does indicate that there can be relatively stable and enduring integrations of the individual themes en route. Thus, in addition to the "peak experience" in which one temporarily experiences personal integration, there are the more perma-

nent integrations that an individual achieves by confronting life's inevitable crises. These more modest integrations need not be disparaged in one's pursuit of ultimate wholeness.

These proposed variations are simply examples. The reader will undoubtedly think of additional possibilities. In making these proposals I have wanted to suggest different types of variations. Some of these variations would involve behavioral changes. The individual would do something to effect personal change. Other variations would involve new insights or understandings. The individual would gain a different understanding of the theme and its meaning for his life. All four themes lend themselves to both types of variations. This is important from the perspective of the pastor who is helping an individual revise or change the characteristic patterns of living, for it suggests that in some cases change will involve variations in behavior and in other cases it will involve variations in insight and understanding. The thematic approach to the study of personality does not limit thematic variations to one or the other of these means of change.

The Case of John Wesley

To make these illustrations of thematic variations more concrete, I conclude this chapter with a case study. While the average congregation could provide numerous cases of individuals oriented around one or another of these four themes, I turn to an important historical figure. The subject is John Wesley, the founder of Methodism. While Wesley's personality reflects elements of all four themes, the dominant theme of his life was resignation. An episode that occurred in the middle period of his life illustrates the influence of this theme on his personality. While Wesley provides a complete account of this episode in his journal, our purposes will be adequately served by a brief summary.[7]

The episode occurred when Wesley served a pastorate in Savannah, Georgia. He had gone to Georgia from his native England in order to convert the Indians. While in Georgia, he became romantically involved with Sophy Hopkey, the niece of an influential Savannah businessman. As this relationship became more serious, Wesley began to consider the possibility of marriage. Miss Hopkey's uncle and aunt seemed to favor the marriage, but Sophy did not encourage Wesley because she had promised another man that she would either marry him or not marry at all. Also, she felt it was best that clergymen not be encumbered with worldly cares. Wesley consulted with Mr. Töltschig, the Moravian pastor, about the matter, but when the latter said he saw no reason why they should not marry, Wesley became more confused than before. He then consulted his friends who had accompanied him to Georgia, and they recommended that he leave town for a few days so that he could think more rationally about it.

He did leave town briefly, but soon he returned to Savannah to transact some business. While there, he longed to see Sophy but restrained the impulse. As he awaited the boat that was to take him away again, Wesley

walked to and fro on the edge of the water, heavy laden and pierced through with many sorrows. There One came to me and said, "You are still in doubt what is best to be done. First, then, cry to God, that you may be wholly resigned, whatever shall appear to be His will." I instantly cried to God for resignation. And I found that and peace together. I said, "Sure it is a dream." I was in a new world. The change was as from death to life. I went back to [the town of] Irene wondering and rejoicing; but withal exceeding fearful, lest my want of thankfulness for this blessing, or of care to improve it, might occasion its being taken away.

When he came back to Savannah three or four days later, he resumed his relationship with Sophy. His friends again warned him against this relationship, that if it continued it could only culminate in marriage. But Sophy's uncle became actively involved by taking Wesley on a tour of the plantation he would provide the couple if they were to marry. If this confused Wesley still more, the crowning blow was struck by Sophy herself. While Wesley was away she had dropped the man she had pledged to marry, but she had begun to see a third man who proposed marriage to her. Wesley learned of this development when Sophy's aunt asked him to publish the banns of marriage for Sophy and her new suitor. Wesley suspected that he had been told of Sophy's relationship to the other man so that he would act before it was too late. But he refused to be pressured. As he put it, "I reasoned thus, 'Either she is engaged or not; if she is, I would not have her if I might: if not, there is nothing in this show which ought to alter my preceding resolution.'"

The next time he saw Sophy she was with her new suitor. While this meeting caused him an almost indescribable "complication of passions and tumult of thought," he sought to treat the occasion as a pastoral visit in which he exhorted Sophy and her suitor to "assist each other in serving God with all their strength." When he returned home he went into his garden and walked up and down, seeking rest but not finding it:

I did seek after God, but I found Him not. I forsook Him before: now he forsook me. I could not pray. Then indeed the snares of death were about me; the pains of hell overtook me. Yet I struggled for life; and though I had neither words nor thoughts, I lifted up my eyes to the Prince that is highly exalted, and supplied the place of them as I could: and about four o'clock He so far took the cup from me that I drank so deeply of it no more.

Wesley immediately wrote Sophy's uncle a note indicating his mind was settled; he would not marry Sophy under any conditions. Her uncle came to Wesley's home within the hour, informing him that he had not yet consented to the marriage. Wesley did not relent. Later that evening Sophy came to Wesley's house for a prayer meeting. After the others had gone, Wesley confronted her, "Miss Sophy, you said yesterday you would take no steps in anything of importance without first consulting me." She replied that she had little choice but to marry her new suitor because she could no longer stand living in the same house with her uncle and aunt. Just then, her suitor entered the house and abruptly took her away.

The following morning Wesley went to see Sophy. He asked her if she was now fully resolved to marry the other man. When she said that she was, he admonished her not to marry for the wrong motives. He pointed out that marrying merely to avoid other problems is not a good motive, because these other problems would continue to plague her in the married state. Having said this, he went home "easy and satisfied." The following day Sophy set out for a neighboring town and was married there by another minister.

After Sophy and her husband settled down to married life in Savannah, Wesley refused Sophy the Sacraments because she had not been faithful in her Christian obligations. This created a major controversy in the church. Sophy's uncle took Wesley to court, but before he was brought to trial, Wesley and his friends left Savannah in the dead of night and sailed back to England. Wesley's famous conversion, commonly referred to as the "Aldersgate experience," occurred three months after his return to England.

Let us now consider this episode in terms of the theme of resignation. While this episode could be interpreted in considerable detail, the following points focus directly on the resignation theme:

1. Wesley was convinced that only one avenue of conflict resolution was open to him. He had to choose between two courses of action. He could either follow his emotions and desires and marry Sophy, or he could honor his calling as a minister and not marry her. When Mr. Töltschig, the Moravian pastor, suggested in effect that he could have it both ways, he left the pastor's office bewildered and confused.

2. Wesley sought confirmation from God that events were proceeding in accord with His will. Divine disclosures, such as the experiences on the beach and in his garden, were valuable but not entirely convincing sources of confirmation that the course he was taking was right.

3. Wesley tends to gain a greater sense of self-control as the episode progresses. Relinquishing Sophy caused intense personal pain and anguish, but not as intense as the uncertainty

he experienced before he resolved the conflict in his own mind. In the later stages of the episode, he is able to withstand considerable pressure to give in to his emotions.[8]

4. Wesley's self-control was reflected in his tendency to fall back on his professional role. In his relations with Sophy after being told she might marry another man, he was able to use the fact that he was Sophy's pastor to disguise and fend off his emotional responses to what was happening. Furthermore, after the marriage he seems to have used his professional role in a vindictive manner. This would indicate that his resignation to what had happened was not complete.

Other observations could be made, but these four are sufficient to enable us to address the issue of variations on the theme of resignation. The question is whether this experience would have made a greater contribution to Wesley's personal growth if there had been variations on this theme? If so, what might these variations be? In attempting to answer this question, I would emphasize that the legitimacy of the resignation theme itself is not being questioned here. Some readers of this account question the very assumptions on which the resignation theme is based. They challenge Wesley's view that he had to choose between Sophy and his career. In a sense, Mr. Töltschig also challenged this view when he suggested that Wesley need not choose between two sets of interests but could honor both. Wesley's inability to accept this suggestion and the confusion and bewilderment it caused indicates how deeply rooted the theme of resignation was in his personality structure. To suggest that he could have both Sophy and his career would be tantamount to saying that his personality should be oriented around the theme of integration rather than the theme of resignation. Thus, our concern is not to argue that Wesley ought to have married Sophy and continued in his ministry. Instead, our question is whether certain variations on the resignation theme would have enabled this experience to make a greater contribution to Wesley's personal growth.

This question directs our attention to our second, third, and fourth observations above. While Wesley was reasonably certain that he was taking the right course of action in not agreeing to marry Sophy, he sought some assurance from God that this was in fact the case. Two unique experiences—at the beach and in his garden—brought assurance that he was acting according to God's will. But in each case these assurances were only partially successful. After each, his strong resolve to forget about Sophy wavered. Thus, these experiences did not give him the self-control that he needed in order to resist the pressure to marry Sophy. He consequently fell back on his professional role and used his office as Sophy's pastor to provide self-control against his unruly passions. Then, as we have noted, he subsequently used his professional prerogatives as her pastor to act vindictively toward her. Readers of Wesley's account of this experience are usually quite critical of his vindictiveness toward Sophy. What they fail to recognize is that throughout the episode he used his professional role to maintain personal self-control, and that his vindictiveness was simply an extension of this use of his professional role.

The question is: Should a minister use his professional role to maintain an otherwise insecure sense of self-control? Should his professional role be a means of maintaining an incongruity between outward demeanor and inner emotions? Should the professional role be allowed to inhibit the minister from exploring his deeper emotions? Is this the ministerial model that he wanted to preserve by not marrying Sophy?

Answers to these questions are not simple, but I would argue that the variation on the theme of resignation needs to relate directly to Wesley's exercise of his professional role. Earlier we noted that one variation on the resignation theme might involve reworking the experience to recover certain positive features of the course of action not taken. In Wesley's case, such a reworking might involve a reappropriation of those aspects of the experience over which he lacked self-control. These were the times when he could not control his emotions. For example, there was his utter confusion on leaving Pastor Töltschig's office, or his deep hurt on being informed that Sophy had decided to marry someone else. These emotions are not simply unruly passions. They are profoundly self-revealing emotions that are thoroughly worthy of informing his ministerial role. If these emotions were not simply renounced in favor of a demeanor of strong self-control, but were instead allowed to inform his understanding of ministry, he would be likely to respond more sensitively and helpfully in the future to parishioners who, like Sophy Hopkey, are experiencing confusion and personal hurt. If Wesley could have reclaimed his emotions, a significant step would have been taken toward positive personal growth.

In concluding this assessment of the Georgia episode, I would emphasize that it is merely an illustration of the thematic approach to human personality. It is not an attempt to psychoanalyze Wesley, nor does it pretend to be a complete thematic interpretation of his personality. It centers on only one theme in Wesley's life and looks at this theme at only one stage in his personal development. I have not selected this particular episode in order to place Wesley in a bad light. In fact, our analysis places him in a better light than many of his staunch supporters claim for him. While I have been critical of his use of his professional role in this episode, I have not challenged the wisdom of his decision not to marry Sophy Hopkey, nor have I challenged his rationale for this decision. Those who do challenge this decision and its rationale are implicitly viewing him from the perspective and assumptions of the theme of integration. Wesley simply does not work out of that particular theme, and there is no ultimate reason why he should. Many of his supporters acknowledge that Wesley was a failure in his personal life, especially in his dealings with women, and the Georgia episode is taken to be a good example of this. But our analysis suggests that his resolution of his conflict over Sophy was not misguided or irrational. The real issue is not that he could not manage his personal life, but that his professional demeanor reflected insensitivity to the deeper needs of the people in his charge. Whether this insensitivity was due solely to his intense personal involvement in this particular situation and was atypical of his professional style cannot be judged on the basis of a single episode. But we *can* say that it is in the area of his professional identity that there is need for personal change.

Conclusion

In developing this thematic analysis of Wesley's experience in Georgia, I am conscious that it is one thing to engage in armchair psychologizing about a historical figure and quite another to be faced with real live persons in one's daily ministry. Is it really practical to suggest that the typical pastor can use the concept of theme in his ministry to individuals? Can the pastor actually identify the enduring themes of individual parishioners and thereby contribute to positive personality change?

I am confident that the thematic approach can be used effectively in ministry to individuals for two reasons. First, the pastor relates to parishioners over extended periods of time and often in quite personal situations (e.g., childbirth, marriage, bereavement, family crises, personal illness). This prompts me to believe that the pastor is afforded a unique opportunity to identify the enduring thematic structures of parishioners' personalities. Indeed, I would argue that most pastors have engaged in something like this task without calling it thematic analysis. If so, I have been providing a theoretical structure for a practical activity in which many pastors already engage. A major purpose of this theoretical structure is to help pastors become more self-conscious in their use of this type of analysis.

Second, I am confident that the thematic approach can be used effectively by pastors in their ministry to individuals because pastors, as a group, are capable of adapting psychological theories and ideas to the specific needs of their own ministries. The thematic approach to human personality is especially amenable to such adaptations. This is one of the primary reasons that Erikson's work has been extensively used in seminary instruction in pastoral care. This chapter indicates that not only Erikson's work in particular, but also the thematic perspective in general, is quite adaptable to the pastoral setting. It also suggests that this thematic perspective is particularly adaptable to the objectives of those pastors who want to help their parishioners effect personal change but not at the expense of ignoring the positive aspects of established personality structures.

2
Psychosocial Themes
in the Local Church

MINISTERS, as a group, are quite capable of adapting ideas developed in other settings for their own ministries. If this is so, the thematic approach to the study of the human personality is especially amenable to such adaptations. Erikson's concept of theme, as developed in his life cycle theory, is an excellent case in point. He himself has made numerous applications of the theory to contexts outside of psychology. Most notable are his applications of the theory to historical figures such as Martin Luther and Mahatma Gandhi.[9] He has also applied the theory to the study of the rituals of American Indians.[10] These examples clearly indicate the usefulness of his theories beyond the boundaries within which psychologists normally work.

Erikson's study of the rituals of American Indians invites us to adapt these themes to the local congregation. He suggests that the sun dance ritual of the Dakota Sioux reflects the psychosocial theme of trust vs. mistrust, thereby providing us with a model for using specific psychosocial themes to identify the characteristic patterns of a local congregation.[11]

To apply psychosocial themes to the local congregation is not as farfetched as it may seem at first glance. For if themes are genuinely psychosocial, they will reflect interactions not only between individuals but also between individuals and social groups. And, if they reflect interactions between individuals and social groups, we would expect the themes not only to reflect individual personalities but also the "personality" of the group. One reason that an individual will join one group rather than another is that the group has a "personality" compatible with his own. It is rather difficult to explain what this group personality is, but pastors and parishioners frequently attest to its existence in local parishes. Erikson's psychosocial themes provide one means of saying something more precise about our intuitive sense that a local church has its own unique personality.

The key to this application of psychosocial themes to the local church is Erikson's suggestion that individual personalities are oriented around a specific psychosocial theme. There are two ways in which this orientation can occur. First, the individual may be oriented around a theme that is currently being experienced as a predominant "crisis" in his life. The adolescent who is currently experiencing an "identity crisis" is strongly oriented around the theme of identity vs. identity diffusion. When he grows beyond this stage, this theme may decrease in importance because it is no longer "critical" to him. Second, the individual may be oriented around a particular theme because it has had an enduring influence on his personality. An individual may, for example, be particularly reflective of the theme of autonomy vs. shame and self-doubt. This individual may have a strong and enduring interest in personal autonomy, but this interest is continually frustrated by an especially pervasive sense of self-doubt. He would like to go beyond the boundaries that he has established or others have established for him, but he inwardly doubts that he is capable of handling the responsibilities that would accompany this freedom. Thus, throughout his life, he is always on the verge of pressing beyond these quite arbitrary limits, but each time something happens to restrain him.

If it is true that the personality of an individual may be strongly oriented around a particular psychosocial theme, then it may be the case that the "personality" of a local congregation is also strongly reflective of a particular psychosocial theme. Like the individual, it may reflect this theme because it is undergoing a "crisis" in its development or because this theme has had a strong influence in the church's development over a longer period of time.

In the final chapter, we will take a close look at a local congregation that is currently experiencing a severe crisis in its development, and we will attempt to apply Erikson's psychosocial themes to it. In this chapter, we focus on two local congregations in which the more enduring influence of specific psychosocial themes is at issue. Both were experiencing difficulties in shaping their dominant psychosocial theme into a unique and creative institutional style. The two cases focus on the minister's roles in directing their churches toward this unique and creative institutional style. The first case is historical; the second contemporary.

The Case of Northampton Parish

This case is based on Richard L. Bushman's analysis of Jonathan Edwards' role as pastor of Northampton parish during the Great Awakening.[12] In focusing on Edwards' pastoral activities and the way they were received in the church at Northampton, Bushman places considerable emphasis on the psychosocial theme of *identity vs. identity diffusion.* He first focuses on Edwards' own conflicts relating to this theme, and then explores the church's struggles with the same theme. His analysis of Edwards' identity conflicts relies heavily on an early essay written by Edwards on the subject of insects. This essay, written when Edwards was only twelve years old, predates his identity crisis. But Bushman contends that it "reflects the tensions" of Edwards' identity struggles in his late teens and early twenties. He also recognizes that the essay is not autobiographical; it is about insects. But he recommends reading the essay as an "unconscious allegory" of human existence, a suggestion that is not farfetched considering that Edwards, in his preaching ministry, made the spider the emblem of man's spiritual plight. In this unconscious allegory, Edwards developed three themes that Bushman considers central both to Edwards' personal psychosocial theme of identity, and to that of the Northampton parish.

The first narrative theme is that *rising leads eventually to destruction.* Young Edwards notices how spiders emit a fine web that carries them upward, floating higher and higher toward the sun. There is considerable pleasure for the spider in this ascent, but, sadly enough, these pleasures prove short-lived. As the spiders mount toward the sun, they are caught in the winds and carried out to sea. There they join other insects and suffer the same violent end, burial in the ocean. Thus, the pleasant rise toward the sun leads to eventual destruction.

A second narrative theme is *vileness under attractive appearances.* While the spider gives the appearance of sagacity and effectiveness, its violent burial at sea is warranted because, beneath its pleasant appearance, the spider gives off nauseous vapors. If large numbers of spiders were to die inland in winter, their smell would be unendurable. Thus, under attractive appearances, the spider conceals its essential vileness.

A third narrative theme is that spiders are *ill-disposed to being manipulated.* Edwards notices that spiders are very sensitive to being jarred by the experimenter and, when jostled, quickly spin a web and drift off. They possess a delicate nervous system that causes them to resist manipulation and close contact with other beings.

In Bushman's view, young Edwards was actually describing his own identity conflicts through these three themes. Thus: (1) Edwards aspired to fulfill high family expectations; but (2) the pleasure and excitement of success was counterbalanced by a fear of destruction due to inward corruption; and (3) his tendency to be fretful and uneasy around other people made close personal relationships hard to sustain. While the psychodynamic origins of these themes in Edwards' earlier childhood are difficult to determine, it appears that the first theme of high aspirations was influenced by the fact that Edwards' maternal forebears were extremely prominent leaders in Puritan New England. Much was expected of the only son of one of the Stoddard daughters. The second theme of the sense of vileness underneath attractive appearances may have its motivational roots in the fact that Edwards' father was a minister. It was incumbent on his family to maintain public respectability whatever the domestic reality. The third theme of tenuous relations with other people may have had its psychodynamic origins in the fact that Jonathan was the only son among ten sisters. While this situation undoubtedly afforded him considerable attention and perhaps solicitude by his sisters, it also prompted the desire to escape from the omnipresence of others.

Bushman contends that Edwards' identity struggles in his later teens and early twenties enabled him to address these identity themes and to resolve most of the personal conflicts they represented. Concerning high aspirations, he relinquished his desire to excel intellectually. He gave up his dream of becoming a philosopher with a European reputation, and he accepted the fact that he would follow in the footsteps of his minister father. Concerning the second theme, an illumination experience generally considered a religious conversion gave him a sense of the purity and loveliness of God. This replaced his inner sense of uncleanliness with new "delights" of a "pure, soul-animating and refreshing nature." With regard to the third theme, he overcame to some extent his uneasiness around people. He still envisioned himself "alone in the mountains, or some solitary wilderness, far from all mankind, sweetly conversing with Christ, and wrapt and swallowed up in God." But he now began to value loving relationships with other committed Christians. In another poetic vision, he pictured the soul of a true Christian as "a little white flower" standing "peacefully and lovingly, in the midst of other flowers round about." It is noteworthy that his identity struggles came to a crisis when he was living in New York City with two saintly people with whom he held intimate discussions on spiritual matters.

In short, Edwards' identity struggles involved coming to terms with the narrative themes developed years earlier in his essay on insects. Now, there is less concern with intellectual superiority, a heightened sense of inner purity and calm, and greater openness to relationships with other persons. The old themes remain central, but there are new variations on these themes.

Bushman shows how these themes and their variations were also central to the personality structure of Edwards' congregation. In his view, Edwards was an effective pastor for more than a decade because of the "emotional congruities of his life and his people's." His personal themes of identity were directly related to the corporate themes of the congregation. Thus, corresponding to his own high aspirations in intellectual endeavors, parishioners entertained high aspirations of economic and social success: "Examples multiplied of small storekeepers who became wealthy merchants and of thrifty farmers who doubled their estates through speculation." But this economic situation was highly volatile. Dramatic success was often followed by destruction: "Commercial and agricultural expansion depended heavily on risk-laden speculations: natural disasters, debt foreclosures, and unforeseen calamities of various kinds could wipe out farmers and traders." In this highly unstable economic climate, increasing attention was paid to the sense of internal corruption underneath appearances of economic and social success. A second corporate theme, then, was reflected in this fact: the average parishioner could not take solace in the proposition that personal success demonstrated divine favor. "At one moment he rested in the assurance of his virtuous diligence and of the prosperity heaven had bestowed. At the next a warning from the pulpit started fears that the lust for gold had hopelessly corrupted his soul." This uncertainty, in turn, led to a third corporate theme. Relationships between neighbors and friends became increasingly brittle: "Economic expansion increased occasions for misunderstanding and ill feeling. The competition for land and trade and for every conceivable economic advantage made enemies of former friends. . . . Even relations with neighbors deteriorated as expansion multiplied the occasions for hard feelings."

Thus, the same themes with which Edwards had struggled personally were prominent features of the corporate life of his congregation. Through his pastorate, his church moved toward the same variations on the themes that he had experienced personally in his identity struggles. Parishioners renounced their economic ambitions. They acknowledged their inner impurity and, through these acknowledgments, gained a new sense of inner calm and divine acceptance. And they pledged neither to defraud their neighbors, default on debts, nor feed a spirit of bitterness, ridicule, and ill will. In this way, the corporate themes of Edwards' congregation correlated with his own personal themes. Because he had worked through to new variations on these personal themes, he was able to support his congregation's readiness for similar variations on its corporate themes.

It should be noted, however, that personal and corporate themes do not always fit this well. Oftentimes, there are marked differences between the personal themes of the pastor and the corporate themes of the congregation. If this were not the case, it would be impossible to thematize fundamental conflicts between the thematic patterns of individuals and the social institutions with which they interact. In fact, Bushman points out that Edwards was eventually forced out of Northampton parish ten years after he assumed the pastorate there because he demanded more "saintliness" from his parishioners than they deemed acceptable. It is not difficult to see how this rupture between parish and pastor might be interpreted in terms of the same themes that were operative earlier. Such an interpretation would focus on the third personal and corporate theme, involving closer and more constructive interpersonal relationships. It would appear that the variations on this theme had less support at the corporate level, even as it had been most difficult for Edwards to realize a variation on this theme at the personal level. His essay on spiders indicated that difficulties in establishing close interpersonal relationships are due to resistance to manipulation. Perhaps, in his demand for saintliness greater than his congregation could muster, Edwards had reverted back to the grand experimenter (manipulating his people) instead of continuing to be the great awakener (evoking hidden qualities). As young Edwards discovered in his study of spiders, the urge to manipulate the object of one's attention becomes almost irresistible when that object threatens to drift away from one's orbit of influence. Presumably this is what happened with Edwards and the Northampton parish.

Bushman's study of Edwards enables us to see how psychosocial themes clarify the interaction of the pastor and his local congregation. Bushman shows how Edwards' own personal themes corresponded to the corporate themes of the congregation, and how his own realization of variations on these themes enabled him to be sensitive to his congregation's readiness for similar variations. We also saw that certain variations may prove more permanent than others, that the institutional changes based on these variations are more secure in some cases than others.

We now shift our vantage point to look at psychosocial themes in the contemporary congregational setting. In the following illustration, we will be considering a modern pastor in a fairly typical modern congregation. In this case, we will not begin with the personal themes of the pastor but will focus exclusively on the corporate themes of the congregation. This will enable us to use Erikson's psychosocial themes to analyze a congregation without making a corresponding analysis of the personality of the pastor. If Erikson's psychosocial themes are applicable to the local congregation, it should be possible to use them simply to identify corporate themes and leave to one side the question of whether the themes correlate with the personal themes of the pastor. The result will be a thematic profile of the congregation.

The Case of Ridge Park Presbyterian Church

The case chosen to illustrate the role of psychosocial themes in the contemporary local church is taken from Evans and Parker's *Christian Theology: A Case Method Approach.*[13] Each of the cases in this book is accompanied by brief theological analyses of the case written by prominent theologians. The case to be discussed here is hypothetical, but quite typical of conflicts encountered in the local parish. It involves a conflict between Elder John Bowles and Pastor Bob Cornwall over the church's priorities.

The pastor has decided to throw his influence behind a struggling evangelism program, an action to which Bowles takes vigorous exception because of what he considers the pastor's heavy-handed methods in attempting to gain support for this program. Cornwall counters that Bowles's complaints about the methods he has employed are motivated by guilt. He suggests that Bowles feels guilty for not supporting the program and these complaints are therefore his way of throwing the onus of guilt onto someone else. Cornwall strongly implies in his next sermon that some members of the congregation are carrying a weight of guilt for their attitudes toward one another. He then invites those who are genuinely aware of God's forgiveness to participate in the Sacrament of the Lord's Supper. Bowles is now faced with the agonizing dilemma of whether to partake of Communion and thus implicitly acknowledge his guilt, or to refuse Communion on the grounds that the pastor has placed inappropriate conditions on his reception of the Sacrament. His mind turns over the events of the previous week as the Communion service proceeds:

1. *Events of the previous Sunday.* "John Bowles remembered [how] last Sunday he . . . had thought through the work of the new Session committee set up to develop the Outreach program. He respected the leaders who had become involved in this program and appreciated what they were doing, but felt that the strong community-oriented projects in the church were more fitting to his own personal style of service.

John saw this emphasis on evangelism as a definite shift in the direction of the Ridge Park Church which was noted throughout the community for its long-standing involvement in social action programs. Many of the church's members were leaders in various community organizations and a substantial number in the congregation were engaged in tutorial programs in two inner-city schools and in an emergency food supply program related directly to the church. The church building was open for various political candidates prior to elections, and to gay and lesbian groups who often had difficulty finding a place to meet. John and Susan Bowles had initially been attracted to Ridge Park because of its style of open service to the community.

Pastor Bob Cornwall, who had first served for a year as an assistant and, following the death of the senior minister, as the pastor of the church for nearly three years, had been an eager supporter of the social action projects of the church. However, he had also sought to support the Session practice of designating annual priorities for ministry and mission. This past January the Session had responded to the enthusiastic request of about six members that the goal for the year be evangelism.

The goal was adopted at the annual congregational meeting the end of January. Following this, a committee of Session had been working very hard on special classes and weekly evening meetings, studying how the church could reach more people in their inner-city community. There had been announcements each Sunday by the committee members about their meetings. These meetings were concluded by teams of church members going calling on residents of the neighborhood who had visited the church in the past. The general response of the congregation to the work of this committee, in their judgment, had been poor. Only a handful of the 200 members of the congregation were actively involved in the program.

With this in mind Pastor Cornwall [had] decided to take the work of the Outreach Committee more directly to the congregation than he had in the past. Following his sermon on the mission of the Church, he reminded the congregation of the notices on "calling" that particular Sunday which had been in the newsletter and in the bulletin for the past two weeks. When the service was over that morning everyone was expected to gather at the back of the sanctuary and go out in teams of two or three to call on residents in the community, distributing brochures on the work of the church. In his benediction Bob Cornwall had prayed that each of the Christians present would take Christ's commission seriously. He concluded by saying there was "no excuse for anyone able-bodied enough to be in church this morning not to go calling after the service." About 10 percent of the congregation, including some visitors, responded to the pastor's request.

2. *Wednesday's Session meeting.* During the Session meeting the following Wednesday, five of the twelve elders [had] expressed their

anger at the way Cornwall had conducted the Sunday service. John Bowles turned to Pastor Cornwall. "There are legitimate reasons why some members of this congregation are unwilling to go calling in the community. I'm a Presbyterian, not Pentecostal; my faith is too precious and private a matter to be foisted on unsuspecting and perhaps unwilling strangers. But my real unhappiness with Sunday's sermon and closing prayer is the clear impression you gave that there is something wrong with the faith of those who didn't go calling in the community. I, for one, had other very definite plans for Sunday afternoon, but even if I hadn't, it should have been perfectly all right for me to decide that I didn't want to go calling. We shouldn't be asked to spread the Word out of guilt, but out of joy. You made everyone who was unable or unwilling to go out feel guilty about not going."

Bob Cornwall responded slowly, "That's not my projection of guilt. It's yours. Four months ago Session voted evangelism as a mission priority and the primary goal of our church year. As your pastor I am taking that goal seriously. Some of you need to think about why you were so disturbed with that call to go and visit in the community and about why you felt guilty when you didn't go. I'm not suggesting for a minute that you have to stand on a soapbox and proclaim the gospel in order to be a part of the Christian community. But as Christians we must have a willingness to put some actions behind our convictions. An integral part of our ministry to one another is to share God's love and the knowledge of that love with others. However, I am equally convinced that in Christ's love we are forgiven even when we are unable or unwilling to see his will in our lives."

3. *To commune or not?* With that note Bob Cornwall [had] called for the next committee report. The subject of evangelism was not discussed again that evening. The next time John Bowles heard about the issue was in church this Sunday morning. John felt that Pastor Cornwall was clearly referring in his comments on forgiveness to the criticism he had received not only from members of the Session but from other members of the congregation who had been offended by the style of last Sunday's service.

John looked up as Bob Cornwall began to distribute the elements to the assisting elders. The pastor was the only one present allowed to administer the Sacrament to the congregation. John felt that Cornwall was using his authority to interpret the spirit with which a Christian could accept the Sacrament. John Bowles was firmly convinced that the experience of worshiping together and sharing the Sacrament of the Lord's Supper was basic to his own spiritual health and to the wholeness of the congregation. If he accepted the Eucharist under Cornwall's stipulation of "forgiveness of guilt," he would be agreeing with the pastor's view that his guilt feelings about calling were tied to an unwillingness to do God's will—in this case specifically related to going calling in the community. He had no doubt that he needed God's forgiveness for his stubbornness, his "hardness of heart." But he felt that if he accepted the Sacrament under the conditions he saw Cornwall putting down, he would be acknowledging that he needed forgiveness on this specific issue . . . that he had done something "wrong" in not feeling that he could or should go calling in the community. The elder handed the plate of wafers to John with the words, "This is Christ's body, broken for you."

Theological issues. Before we develop our own thematic assessment of Ridge Park Church, we can gain valuable insight into this case by looking at the brief interpretations written by three prominent theologians.[14] The authors of these theological interpretations do not agree on every facet of the case, and they were not under any pressure by the editors of the book to reach a consensus. On the immediate question of whether John Bowles should take Communion, the first theologian says that Bowles ought not receive it "at this ritual moment" because his refusal can be "a movement in the process to confront Bob Cornwall and John's fellow elders with the need to examine critically their image of the Church and its implications for the Church's purpose and mission." The second theologian says that Bowles ought to receive the Lord's Supper on the grounds that he was not convinced in his conscience that he had sinned in this case; he was therefore spiritually ready to receive the Sacrament. The third writer suggests that Bowles's decision in this regard depends on his ability to receive the Sacrament "as the sign and instrument of God's forgiveness of the sins of which he is honestly aware" and "of his fellowship with Pastor Cornwall in spite of their differences." Thus, there is no clear unanimity on this immediate question of whether Bowles should commune or not. There are also different interpretations of the attitudes and motives of the individuals involved. But, in spite of these differences, there is considerable agreement as to what are the major pastoral issues raised by this episode. These issues, and the theologians' handling of these issues, can be summarized as follows:

1. *The purpose of the church.* The theologians agree that what is basically at issue here is the purpose or mission of the church. The second of the three theologians expresses the view that the church is "to be understood more as means than as end, more as servant than as privileged center of God's saving presence and activity. The Church's mission is more than word-and-sacrament. It is committed as well to the pursuit of justice and the transformation of the world." The first theologian shares the view that the church is not an end in itself, but suggests that there is too much emphasis on the church as "means" in this case and not enough on the church as community:

Thus a Bob Cornwall or a John Bowles evaluates the significance of his community of faith on the basis of its production for, and impact on, the wider society in which the Church exists. Talk about specific tasks, sometimes disguised under mission goals, plunges the Church into goal-setting, not as the natural consequence of life together but as that which controls the rhythm of corporate existence as members of Christ's body.[15]

The third theologian deals with the question of purpose by distinguishing between lay and ordained leadership. How does this division of roles advance or impede the church's accomplishment of its mission, especially in the specific area of evangelism?

2. *The minister's style of leadership.* The theologians generally agree that Bob Cornwall has a tendency to operate in a coercive manner. The first theologian puts it this way: "Bob Cornwall sees the priority of evangelism in terms of a program in which most, if not all, members of the community *must* engage if they are to be faithful to the Church." The second

says that "Cornwall exceeded the limits of pastoral propriety by apparently adopting a course of spiritual intimidation. To insist that there could be 'no excuse' for any member of the congregation not to go out and call upon nonmembers that same afternoon is presumptuous at best, overbearing at worst, and naive in any case." The third theologian attributes the conflict at Ridge Park Presbyterian to Cornwall's style of leadership: "The dissension in the Ridge Park congregation derives largely from Pastor Cornwall's style of leadership. He is a strong leader, going out ahead of his people and pulling them firmly in what he believes is the right direction in the mission of the Church." The same writer feels so strongly that Cornwall's style of leadership is inappropriate that he recommends: "The Session must also take up with Pastor Cornwall his style of leadership and ask him to consider whether it has been improperly coercive." The three theologians are also agreed that Cornwall's style of leadership and the Ridge Park congregation's understanding of the church's purposes are deeply related. The first writer points out, for example, that the charge that Bob Cornwall contrived "guilt feelings among his congregation in order to promote a program of evangelism" reflects an "ambiguity in their image of the Church."

3. *The inappropriateness of the dissident elders' reactions.* There is general agreement that if Pastor Cornwall was too coercive, his lay leaders were either overreacting or insufficiently attentive to their responsibility to be supportive of the pastor. On the *overreacting* issue, the second writer points out that the "pastor did not explicitly connect the need 'to accept God's forgiveness for (their) guilt' and the lack of cooperation of most members with the parish's 'Operation Outreach.' " He also points out that "Pastor Cornwall never suggested that the congregation should spread the Word of the Lord 'out of guilt,' his intimidating manner notwithstanding." On the *supportive* issue, the same writer points out that Cornwall was not replacing the church's social action program with the evangelism program, but merely augmenting the church's existing programs. Furthermore, Cornwall was attempting to be responsive

to the decisions of the Session and the annual congregational meeting, and this "was a legitimate, and indeed necessary, predisposition on the part of any pastoral leader with a sense of accountability to his congregation." The other two writers believe that the elders have a responsibility to be supportive, but they question whether this simply means committing themselves to the evangelism program. The first theologian suggests that the minister and Elder Bowles both conceive the church's purpose in excessively task-oriented terms, and that rather than debating the relative merits of evangelism vs. social action, the way Elder Bowles can best be supportive is to challenge the congregation to reach a clearer understanding of itself as a community. In this theologian's judgment, Bowles's refusal to take Communion will escalate the conflict, but he will be acting out of a deeper understanding of the church as community, i.e., as a group that "offers intimate support *combined* with intimate critique." The third theologian raises questions concerning the church's evangelism and social action programs. He points out that Operation Outreach seems to be limited to those who have visited the church in the past; in his judgment, there is no reason except expediency for limiting evangelism in this way. On the other hand, he is also critical of the church's social action program, noting that "most of the programs seem to be of the nature of social service, that is, directly helping those who are in need, rather than social action, that is, working to change the conditions and structures which cause people to be in need in various ways. The mission of the Church must include both of these." The implication here is that Cornwall and Bowles should not get themselves polarized over these two programs, because both programs probably need to be rethought in the light of a more adequate understanding of the church's purpose.

4. *The Sacrament and the problem of guilt.* All three theologians recognize that the issue of guilt plays an important role in the situation. But they differ as to how much importance it has, and as to whether it should be a factor in Bowles's participation in Communion. The second theologian, who pointed

out that Pastor Cornwall did not explicitly relate his sermon on guilt to the evangelism issue, concludes that Bowles's uncertainty as to whether to take Communion is "essentially a problem of his own making." But the third theologian observes that Bowles may not feel guilty about not going calling on nonmembers, but he has other sins of which he is "honestly aware" and ought therefore to receive the Sacrament as the "sign and instrument of God's forgiveness" of these sins. The first theologian views the issue of guilt as largely a factor in Cornwall's coercive style; Cornwall does not seem to shy away from using guilt to motivate his parishioners. But this writer does not consider guilt a central issue in whether Bowles should participate in the Sacrament. In his view, Bowles's decision here is not a question of whether he is guilty or not, or whether he acknowledges his guilt or not, but what his decision about taking Communion will achieve in terms of the church's larger purposes. Thus, there is considerable variation among the theologians as to how much weight to give this issue of guilt: Is Bowles correct in his assumption that Cornwall's public references to guilt are directly related to the evangelism issue? Whether Cornwall linked these two issues or not, is Bowles right to consider them to be unrelated? Should his conviction that Cornwall is using guilt coercively affect his full participation in the worship service?

The psychosocial theme of initiative vs. guilt. Having summarized the major pastoral issues raised by the theologians, we may proceed to our own thematic analysis of this case. This analysis is not meant to supplant the theological interpretations of the case. At the same time, it is not merely supplementary in the sense that it only fills in the gaps that the theological interpretations were unable to fill. The thematic analysis based on psychosocial themes is a valid perspective in its own right. The question is whether the two perspectives together are able to come to a more adequate understanding of the case, and thus of the congregation, than either one of them separately.

Our analysis is based on Erikson's psychosocial theme of *initiative vs. guilt.* This analysis is based on Erikson's descrip-

tion of the initiative vs. guilt theme in his essay "Growth and
Crises of the Healthy Personality." It also draws from his essay
"Human Strength and the Cycle of Generations," in which he
develops a *schedule of virtues* to correspond to the life stages.[16]
In view of the theologians' emphasis on the issue of the
church's purpose, it is noteworthy that the virtue that corresponds to the initiative vs. guilt theme is that of *purpose*. (See
diagram on p. 63).

In somewhat the same manner that Bushman identified
specific narrative themes in Edwards' struggle with the theme
of identity vs. identity diffusion, we will identify some of the
narrative themes in Erikson's discussion of the initiative vs.
guilt theme, and show how each has relevance to the Ridge
Park Presbyterian case.

1. *Coercive or constructive intrusion?* Erikson says that the
child's tendency to be intrusive (including physical attack,
aggressive talking, vigorous locomotion, and consuming curiosity) is a dominant behavior of the initiative vs. guilt theme. He
emphasizes that intrusiveness is not in itself an undesirable
form of interaction. But he does warn that it can degenerate
into undesirable modes of behavior if not directed toward
constructive and ultimately peaceful ends. For example, excessive parental restraint on the child's intrusiveness may cause
him to become overly unobtrusive, deeply fearful of the dan-
gers that await him when narrowly defined boundaries are
trespassed. On the other hand, a lack of constructive ends
toward which he is able to direct his energies may lead the child
to become excessively obtrusive, i.e., devoting his energies to
bossing and coercing other people.

This theme of *coercive or constructive intrusion* relates especially to church members' interactions with nonmembers.
Evangelism or outreach is normally the most intrusive form of
initiative in a local church's program. There is much fear
among church people that this intrusiveness may degenerate
into coerciveness. Elder Bowles expresses this concern when he
says that evangelism involves foisting one's faith on unsuspecting and perhaps unwilling strangers. There is much evidence

THE INTERPLAY OF SUCCESSIVE LIFE STAGES

	1	2	3	4	5	6	7	8
H. OLD AGE								Integrity vs. Despair, Disgust: WISDOM
G. MATURITY							Generativity vs. Self-Absorption: CARE	
F. YOUNG ADULTHOOD						Intimacy vs. Isolation: LOVE		
E. ADOLESCENCE					Identity vs. Identity Confusion: FIDELITY			
D. SCHOOL AGE				Industry vs. Inferiority COMPETENCE				
C. PLAY AGE			Initiative vs. Guilt: PURPOSE					
B. EARLY CHILDHOOD		Autonomy vs. Shame, Doubt: WILL						
A. INFANCY	Trust vs. Mistrust: HOPE							

in the history of evangelistic witnessing to warrant this concern. The question, however, is whether Elder Bowles fails to discriminate between constructive and coercive forms of intrusiveness. Does he use the argument that evangelism is likely to be coercive to justify an excessive self-restriction, an extreme unobtrusiveness based on the assumption that expressions of personal faith or commitment to nonmembers are automatically coercive? Undoubtedly, Elder Bowles and the other dissident elders are not alone in taking this view of evangelism. Their feelings about intruding into the lives of other people are probably shared by many other parishioners, including some of those who are directly responsible for implementing the evangelism program.

Another side of this matter of intrusiveness concerns the intrusions that an evangelistic program makes on those who do the evangelizing. In this regard, Elder Bowles is worried not only about intruding on unsuspecting strangers but also about intrusions on his own "precious and private faith." In fact, he seems more concerned about intrusions on his own spiritual life than about intrusions that the evangelism program foists on others. His resentment against Pastor Cornwall is predicated on this very concern. In his judgment, Cornwall's suggestion that the dissident elders felt guilty is an inappropriate intrusion on his own private faith. What right does Cornwall have to say what Bowles's private thoughts and motives are? Thus, for Elder Bowles, the evangelism dispute comes down to this: Does anyone have the right to intrude on the religious lives of others? When we support an evangelism program, we answer this question with a qualified yes. Such intrusions are appropriate if they are directed toward constructive ends. Thus Pastor Cornwall and supporters of the evangelism program might address the issue being raised by Bowles by making more adequate discriminations between constructive and coercive intrusiveness. The failure to make such discriminations usually results in excessive self-restrictions, in an unobtrusiveness that leads church members to fail to take legitimate initiatives toward nonmembers.

Finally, Elder Bowles's objections to the evangelism program have given its supporters an excellent opportunity to test their evangelistic skills. How they handle Elder Bowles's objections here will undoubtedly reveal something of their own capacities as evangelists. Thus, in recommending clearer discriminations between constructive and coercive intrusiveness, I do not merely mean engaging in didactic exercises. Elder Bowles has provided the program's supporters an almost ideal occasion to manifest, in their own responses to these objections, constructive intrusiveness. His concern to protect his faith, to keep it personal and precious, is the same objection that *nonmembers* often raise against involvement in the church. From the evangelists' point of view, this concern to protect the privacy of one's faith needs to be intruded upon. But if this intrusion is constructive rather than coercive, Elder Bowles (and nonmembers) will feel less need to be protective of their faith.

2. *Literal obedience or shared obligations?* In discussing the formation of conscience in the initiative vs. guilt stage, Erikson points out that the child may develop an obedience more literal than the one the parent wishes to exact, and that he may develop lasting resentments because his parents do not live up to the new conscience they have fostered in their child. This problem of a literalistic obedience and an unforgiving attitude toward parents is averted or overcome, however, through experiences in which the child and the parent participate together in shared obligations. Now the parent is not seen as merely a lawgiver, but rather as a co-worker with whom the child participates in carrying out common responsibilities. Through such experiences, the child senses that he shares with his parents "an equality of worth, in spite of the inequality in time schedules."

This theme of *literal obedience vs. shared obligations* is especially reflected in the interaction between the pastor and lay members of the congregation. It comes to overt expression in the interaction between Pastor Cornwall and Elder Bowles. In Bowles's view, Cornwall has transgressed against a very fundamental concept that he has undoubtedly preached upon many times, i.e., that an individual's faith is not to be judged by his actions alone. In Bowles's view, to suggest that one's faith hinges on whether he goes calling Sunday afternoon is to violate a very basic Protestant understanding of justification by faith and not by works. Thus, Cornwall has not lived up to the "new conscience" he has often preached about. We can hear Bowles complaining: When Cornwall speaks in general terms about faith and works, he tells us our faith cannot be judged by our works. But when he gets down to specific situations, he judges our faith by our works. Elder Bowles's resentment is based on his view that Cornwall had earlier fostered a "freer conscience" (i.e., faith does not depend on what we do) but now was seeming to enforce a "stricter conscience." The issue is not the precise range of freedom or restriction that the "parent" had previously established, but rather the parent's transgression in a matter of central importance to both parent and child's basic understanding of their moral obligations to one another. If the parent originally communicates to the child that their relationship is not dependent on the child's performance of certain activities, and then the parent later makes clear that the relationship *does* depend on such performance, his "transgression" against the child is no less serious than if he had performed an act the child is not allowed to perform.

On the other hand, Bowles's relationship to Cornwall is too much predicated on literalistic obedience. His churchmanship seems to reflect an obedience more literal than the pastor wishes to exact. For example, Bowles appears to be taking Cornwall's remarks about the relationship between faith and calling on nonmembers on Sunday afternoon more literally than the pastor intended. If Cornwall implied that his parishioners' faith would hinge on how they spent Sunday afternoon, did he really expect this implication to be taken *that* seriously and *that* personally? Presumably, he expected this implication to be understood within the larger context of his frequent and continuing affirmations of the basic tenet that our faith cannot be judged by our works. Yet, there is a dimension of his leadership style that appears to foster attitudes of literal obedience. He occasionally treats his elders as if there is an "inequality of worth" between pastor and laity. He seems to take advantage of the one real inequality between them (i.e., not the parent's greater chronological age but the minister's leadership role) and turns it into a condition of worth. As Erikson puts it, the parent sometimes engages in a "thoughtless exploitation" of this inequality. There is clear evidence of this thoughtless exploitation in Cornwall's impatient response to the anger expressed toward him at the Session meeting. This response undoubtedly gives Bowles good reason to suspect that the pastor is not above using his privileged role in the organization to exert "arbitrary power" over his parishioners. It also tends to justify Bowles's contention that Cornwall uses the mechanism of guilt in an illegitimate way. It is not that Cornwall uses guilt to coerce people into action (obviously, Bowles did not feel its coercive force in this way, for if he had, he would have been out calling on nonmembers Sunday afternoon); it is that he uses guilt to exploit the inequality in status between himself and his parishioners.

This is not to say that the pastor has no right to point out instances in which his parishioners are guilty. This is appropriately done, however, in the context of equality of worth—as one co-worker to another. Cornwall's condescending tone on Wednesday evening does not convey this sense of equality of worth between himself and his elders. On the contrary, he exploits his inequality of status by "patiently" explaining to his elders that they are projecting their own guilt onto his earlier statements about the importance of the evangelism program. He then reinforces this didactic response to their expressions of anger by adding: "Some of you need to think about why you were so disturbed with that call to go and visit in the community and about why you felt guilty when you didn't go." In effect, he denies any personal responsibility for evoking their sense of guilt, and he suggests that they are not psychologically astute enough to recognize that their anger against him is a projection of their own guilt.

In short, Bowles's attitude throughout the course of this episode reflects a literalistic obedience; this attitude extends from his initial interpretation of Cornwall's remarks on the previous Sunday morning to his current uncertainty about whether he ought to partake of Communion. On the other hand, it also appears that Cornwall has fostered an atmosphere in the church that invites this literalistic form of obedience.

The solution? A variation on this theme of literal obedience vs. shared obligations in which pastor and parishioners cultivate more experiences involving shared obligations. Perhaps there has already been considerable sharing of obligations in co-worker fashion in the church's social action programs. And possibly the issue of evangelism has temporarily diverted the pastor and parishioners from their customary modes of interaction. However, if the pastor's handling of the Session meeting is at all reflective of the way the other programs have been handled, there appears to be a need for more experiences in which pastor and parishioners participate in terms of shared obligations and a co-worker relationship. His summary dismissal of the elders' expressions of anger against him may explain their seeming inconsistency in having voted for evangelism as a mission priority and now belatedly advancing objections against it. If he would not listen to these expressions of anger now, can we assume that he listened to their earlier objections to the program then? Also, if there were more of a co-worker relationship between pastor and laity, instead of attacking Bowles by means of a one-sided psychological analysis ("That's not my projection of guilt. It's yours"), Cornwall could have noted that they both felt some of the same resistance to supporting the evangelism program and both felt guilty about this resistance ("I guess in wanting to say that you are projecting your guilt onto me, I am trying to project my guilt onto you. Maybe we both feel rather guilty about our attitudes toward this evangelism business").[17]

3. *Anticipatory rivalry and free collaboration.* Erikson points out that, in the initiative vs. guilt stage, the child experiences an *"anticipatory rivalry* with those who were there first and who

may therefore occupy with their superior equipment the field toward which one's initiative is directed." Normally expressed against a parent, this rivalry may manifest itself in "embittered and yet essentially futile attempts at demarcating a sphere of unquestioned privilege" and may become a major impetus toward "a final contest for a favored position with one of the parents." The only satisfactory solution to this rivalry is that the younger participant recognizes that he cannot win in any ultimate sense, and that his best course of action is to collaborate with his perceived rival on projects of mutual interest.

The theme of *anticipatory rivalry and free collaboration* is reflected in the interaction of supporters of the social action program vs. the pastor and supporters of the evangelism program. We are told that Bowles and his wife joined Ridge Park Presbyterian because of its emphasis on social action. Now, however, a small group of parishioners has begun to press for an evangelism program. Even though the evangelism program was officially adopted by the Session, it is now clear that some people consider it a competing enterprise, a smaller but potentially powerful rival to the "elder" siblings of the parish and their social action programs. However, while sibling rivalry and its accompanying jealous rage may be a subtheme in this particular aspect of the controversy, a more dominant concern is that the pastor, through his support of the evangelism program, may be divesting parishioners like Elder Bowles of an important "sphere of unquestioned privilege" that they have enjoyed through their engagement in social action programs. The issue, then, is not so much whether the evangelism program itself is a powerful threat to the social action program, but whether Pastor Cornwall has shifted his allegiances to the evangelism program and may allow it to set the church's future direction and purpose.

Elder Bowles and the other dissident elders feel that Pastor Cornwall is favoring the evangelism program. Cornwall implies that every member of the congregation ought to become involved in the evangelism program and, in attempting to get the evangelism program off the ground, seems to slight the efforts of those who have engaged in social action programs for a much longer period of time. If so, then he could well be perceived by the social action advocates as a rival force in the overall purpose and control of the organization. While this sense of rivalry may only be incipient at this time, the evangelism dispute indicates that there could eventually be a more open and hostile struggle over who is in control of the church and its programs.

How can this problem of anticipated rivalry be averted? Pastor Cornwall is undoubtedly right in not bending to pressure to disband the evangelistic program. But it is his responsibility to ensure that neither the evangelism nor the social action advocates rout the other from the field. How to do this is the question. It would do no more good to remind the dissident elders that they voted to support the new evangelism program than to tell a child that he said he wanted a baby brother and is therefore obligated to love the infant. What is needed is concrete assurances from the pastor that the social action program will not be dismantled or neglected in favor of evangelism, and that the traditional thrust of the church toward social action will continue to have priority over the long run. These assurances might be taken to mean that the pastor is merely appeasing evangelism advocates in supporting their initiatives, but they might also have the opposite effect of reducing the dissident elders' anxiety to such an extent that they would volunteer to collaborate with the pastor on the evangelism program. The older child who is secure in his position in the family can replace rivalry toward the infant with care and solicitude. This may result in a two-pronged outreach program that would enable individual parishioners to continue to honor their personal preferences (either evangelism or social action) but to work together within the parameters of these personal dispositions. In this way, the pastor's insistence that both types of programs will receive appropriate attention need not result in a polarization in which everyone loses. It may be the occasion for a new, previously unenvisioned form of collaboration between the two groups of parishioners, and between the social action supporters and the pastor.

Admittedly, this solution sounds terribly idealistic. But unless we assume that the church is an utterly different institution from that of the family, there is considerable evidence from family experience that this resolution of anticipatory rivalry between older child and parent through collaborative activities can and does occur. As Erikson puts it, "there is little in these inner developments which cannot be harnessed to constructive and peaceful initiative if only we learn to understand the conflicts and anxieties" they reflect. As parents are surprised when an older child is threatened by a new baby, Pastor Cornwall and those involved in the evangelism program seem surprised that a program that garners support from only 10 percent of the congregation could cause some elders anxiety. However, their anxiety does not result from their perception of the relative power of the evangelism group as such, but from their fear that the pastor may use the evangelism program (or any other program in which Bowles and the other dissidents are not directly involved) to reduce their influence within the organization. And, while Pastor Cornwall who only three years ago was the associate minister of the church may find this perception of his own potential power equally surprising, Bowles would not have been so frank about his unhappiness with Cornwall's handling of the Sunday service if he did not think the pastor possessed considerable power and influence within the congregation. Bowles's criticism of the pastor is not mere testiness. It expresses his anxiety that he could well be excluded from this sphere of pastoral power and influence, and that he himself might be divested of his own sphere of unquestioned privilege as an elder of the congregation.

4. *Exploratory play and purposeful action.* In considering this narrative theme of exploratory play and purposeful action, we shift our attention to the schedule of virtues that correspond to the life stages. (See diagram on page 63, "The Interplay of Successive Life Stages.") As indicated, the virtue that corresponds to the initiative vs. guilt stage—which Erikson calls the "play age"—is *purpose*. In Erikson's view, the rudi-

ments of purpose are developed in the child's play and fantasy: "Play is to the child what thinking, planning, and blueprinting are to the adult, a trial universe in which conditions are simplified and methods exploratory, so that past failures can be thought through, expectations tested." In addition to being *exploratory,* play is also *anticipatory* because it enables the child "to master the future by anticipating it in countless variations of repetitive themes." From these early explorations and anticipations of the future, the child develops an appreciation for purposeful activity.

This theme of *exploratory play and purposeful action* is best exemplified in the interaction between ritual participants in the church's corporate worship. In a sense, the worship service at Ridge Park Presbyterian was enabling Bowles, Cornwall, and other parishioners to explore and test out the "real purpose" of the church. The theologians are agreed that this case is basically about the church's fundamental purpose. Thus, if the "real business" of the church is conducted in the Session meeting, the playful exploration of the many variations this business might take occurs in the context of the church's corporate worship. In this sense, while Bowles took Pastor Cornwall's statements during the various worship services too literally, he was nonetheless right not to dismiss them as so much pious verbiage, but to recognize that Cornwall was testing out a major variation—evangelism—on the church's corporate themes. And, if Bowles failed to recognize a strong element of fantasy and wishful thinking in Cornwall's "anticipation" that the whole congregation might participate in the Sunday afternoon visitation, he was also right to recognize that in another sense the pastor "meant business." The worship service is play, but in the carefully delimited sense that it is a "trial universe" concerned to assist participants in "mastering the future." It provides an occasion for the church to test its purposes and master certain methods for carrying out these purposes.

On the other hand, Erikson points out that sometimes "an emotion becomes so intense that it defeats playfulness." He calls this *play disruption,* "the sudden and complete or diffused and slowly spreading inability to play."[18] Perhaps Bowles's anxiety concerning Cornwall's handling of the evangelism issue has reached the point where he has no choice but to "disrupt" the action and thereby signal to the other participants how deeply this issue has affected him. This could take the form of refusal of Communion. The disruption would most appropriately occur during Communion because this aspect of the worship service best dramatizes the church's sense of common *purpose*. On the other hand, if he does take Communion and thereby engage in this expression of common purpose, we would hope that this would not be done in a spirit of mere frustration, but that this very act would evoke in Bowles a renewed capacity to *anticipate* new variations on the repetitious pattern that the evangelism conflict has already begun to assume. As noted earlier, Bowles's frame of mind during this episode had taken on a strong tone of literalistic obedience. By thinking more deeply about the symbolic nature of the act of communing, Bowles can relinquish this attitude of literalistic obedience and begin to anticipate a course of more genuinely productive and truly purposeful action in the evangelism controversy.

Initiatives available to Pastor Cornwall. This analysis of the Ridge Park case indicates that conflicts in the local church can be resolved by identifying the principal forms of interaction involved and then determining how to maximize the potential of these forms of interaction for positive resolution of the conflict. By conceiving these forms of interaction in thematic terms, this analysis suggests that the pastor may take the following steps toward this resolution: (1) encourage discrimination between constructive and coercive forms of intrusion in evangelism; (2) use the similarity between Bowles's and nonmembers' anticipated objections to evangelism efforts to assess evangelism skills; (3) work toward a greater sense of sharing obligations as co-workers, thereby reducing the current attitudes of literal obedience; (4) give explicit verbal assurances that the evangelism program will not supplant the established social action programs; (5) make more constructive use of the worship service as a "trial universe." Some of these initiatives could prove effective almost immediately, others may involve long-term nurturance. But virtually any combination of these initiatives would enable Pastor Cornwall and the members of Ridge Park Church to begin to work together in a spirit of common purpose.[19]

Psychosocial Themes and Ministerial Models

In focusing on the Northampton and Ridge Park churches, we have seen how a particular psychosocial theme can shape the "personality" of a local congregation. In concluding our thematic approach to the local congregation, I would like to augment these two illustrations by noting how a dominant psychosocial theme can also be reflected in the professional style of the minister of a local congregation.

The professional identities of ministers are based on models of ministry. While the minister's professional style reflects his own unique personality, it is also shaped by his adoption of one of the ministerial models provided by the profession itself. These models shape the way that the local minister envisions his work, and they help to define his expectations of the congregation he serves. Four important ministerial models are the mystical, the saintly, the prophetic, and the pastoral. These are not exhaustive of the professional models available to the Christian minister, but they are among the major models that give the ministry its professional identity. The basic thrust of our analysis here is that these four models reflect the psychological interests of the first four stages of the life cycle. Through these four models, the psychosocial themes of infancy and early childhood are a perennial feature of local church life.

The *mystical* model of ministry reflects the trust vs. mistrust theme. The mystic seeks the vision of God in much the same way that the infant seeks to maintain eye contact with the mother. Like the infant, the mystic experiences trust when the object of his devotion can be envisioned, but experiences mistrust—"the dark night of the soul"—when this object is not in view. At such times, the mystic, like the infant, may employ special methods of supplication to recover the presence of God. Thus, this model of ministry may give particular attention to the worship service and other ritual and devotional acts as a means of enabling parishioners to experience trust in the reality of God.

The *saintly* model of ministry reflects the theme of autonomy vs. shame and self-doubt. This theme involves expressing one's will in socially constructive ways. However, when the saint finds himself expressing his autonomy in ways that are opposed to the will of others, he is susceptible to shame and self-doubt. Sometimes, others seek to bring his actions or convictions into conformity with theirs by holding his behavior and views up to ridicule. Other times, he experiences self-doubt when he wonders whether he is merely being obstinate in not following the will of others, or when he questions whether having his own way in these matters is worth the difficulty it causes in his personal and professional relationships. The saintly model of ministry is reflected in the minister's concern to establish a firm (but not necessarily rigid) set of beliefs and moral standards to channel the congregation's autonomy into consistent and constructive patterns of behavior. This may involve, for example, the formation of study groups whose purpose is to help parishioners learn to apply their faith to practical and moral problems of daily living.

The *prophetic* model reflects the theme of initiative vs. guilt. The prophet takes initiatives that test the congregation's existing boundaries, and he often does this with considerable attention to strategic planning. However, the prophet experiences guilt when he fails to meet his purposes and goals, or when he has reason to question whether the highest ethical standards have been maintained in his pursuit of these goals. He agonizes, for example, over whether he has used inappropriate forms of coercion to secure support for his objectives. As we have seen in the Ridge Park Presbyterian case, the initiatives of the prophetic model of ministry may include evangelism as well as social action.

The *pastoral* model of ministry relates to the industry vs. inferiority theme. The pastor assumes his role as a constituent part of a productive solution to problems, and he establishes a work pattern characterized by steady attention and persevering diligence. Thus the positive pole of this ministerial model is effective industry carried out in a spirit of cooperation and willing compromise. However, the pastor experiences a sense of professional inferiority when he encounters situations in which available resources (skills, materials, motivations) are inadequate to cope effectively with the tasks to which the congregation has committed itself. This model of ministry is especially evident in the pastor's steady attention to the development of the congregation's human resources through education and pastoral care.

Though brief and sketchy, these correlations of ministerial models and psychosocial themes have important implications for a thematic understanding of ministry in the local church. For example, these correlations indicate that each model is limited by virtue of its responsiveness to a particular set of psychosocial dynamics. Ministers address this limitation by expanding their professional identity to include more than one of these models. However, to avoid the opposite problem of professional diffusion, ministers will make one model the dominant theme of their ministry and allow the other models to function in differing proportions as variations on this dominant theme.

It is also important to emphasize that all four models recognize the need for institutional change. It is not the case that one model is oriented toward change while another supports maintenance of existing institutional patterns. While it is true that the pastoral model, based on the dynamic of industry and inferiority, is less dramatic than the prophetic models, this does not mean that it is less oriented to change. On the other hand, as with personality change in the individual, little institutional change will be effected by any of these models if the negative pole of the psychosocial theme is ignored. Mistrust, shame and self-doubt, guilt, and inferiority cause congregations to resist the positive change reflected in trust, autonomy, initiative, and industry. But change is most likely to occur when the minister recognizes these sources of resistance to change and treats them with the same respect he accords the positive change factors of trust, autonomy, initiative, and industry. These negative interests need to be taken seriously because, whether acknowledged or ignored, they are part of the unique personality structure of the individual congregation.

Conclusion

The illustrations developed in this chapter indicate that congregations reflect dominant psychosocial themes of a relatively permanent nature. These themes play an influential role in the ongoing life of the church. They reflect where the church has been in the past and help chart where it is going in the future. These institutional themes are not so inflexible, however, that they are not amenable to change. They clearly lend themselves to variations. In the case of Northampton parish, the pastor was able to envision such variations by virtue of his earlier personal struggle with similar themes. In the case of Ridge Park Church, an impasse had been reached where certain variations were needed but had not yet been envisioned, articulated, or implemented. In either case, the pastor's task was not to propose or attempt to implement entirely new thematic structures in the congregation, but to work toward variations on existing themes. As the Northampton case indicates, such variations on existing themes can be as transformative of corporate structures as they are of personality structures. The "great awakening" that Northampton parish experienced was not due to the introduction of totally new psychosocial themes but to variations on existing themes.

These examples, especially the Ridge Park Presbyterian case, also indicate that the variations that are most likely to effect positive change in the congregation are those that are capable of effecting a creative integration of the two dimensions of the theme. The task is not merely to accentuate the positive dimension and eliminate the negative dimension, but to effect an integration of the two that will reflect the church's unique institutional style. The danger that every church confronts is the continuing threat that these two dimensions will disintegrate into mere contradiction. This is the problem that Ridge Park Church is currently facing. The challenge before this congregation is to effect a creative integration not only of the two programs of evangelism and social action but also, and more fundamentally, to integrate its tendencies of initiative and guilt into an effective institutional style. This style will be weighted toward initiative, but not at the expense of ignoring the guilt that members feel—both individually and collectively —as they exercise these initiatives.

Finally, it should be noted that both of our illustrations have focused on a single thematic trend in the congregational profile. Even as individual personalities are influenced by more than one major theme, most congregations reflect more than one influential theme. And sometimes these themes are in conflict with one another. This latter problem will be discussed in the final chapter of this study, where we take up the problem of major crises in the local church setting.

3

The Thematic Approach
to Pastoral Counseling

Thematic Meditation: Precursor
to Pastoral Counseling

In *The Poetry of Meditation,* Louis Martz points to the widespread influence of the *Spiritual Exercises* of Ignatius Loyola.[20] The procedures for meditation set forth in this book were widely used by religious counselors, and for this reason attract our attention here. Originally designed to be performed during a month set aside for intensive meditation, the methods developed in *Spiritual Exercises* were adapted to an hourly time frame. The meditation would begin with a simple prayer and then proceed to the meditation itself.

The first step in the meditation would be to identify the "place" on which the meditation would center. This was called "composition of place" or "seeing the spot." For example, in meditating on the birth of Christ, composition of place would require imagination to reconstruct this event. The meditator would form the figure of some open place without shelter, and a child wrapped in swaddling cloths and lying in a manger. There are three different ways of composing the place or event. The first is to imagine oneself present in the very spot where the event occurred. The second is to imagine the event happening in the very place where the meditation is being carried out. And the third is to internalize the event as though it were happening within one's own heart.

After composition of place, the meditation proceeds to the

three stages of meditation proper, i.e., *memory, understanding,* and *will.* Memory involves recollection of God in relation to the event that is the subject of meditation. Understanding involves forming a true, proper, and thorough concept of the event that is being meditated upon. Will involves acting on the understanding that has been attained. This threefold division of memory, understanding, and will was viewed in Trinitarian terms, with memory relating to the Father, understanding to the Son, and will to the Holy Spirit.

This meditation structure underwent considerable refinement in the years following the initial impact of *Spiritual Exercises.* One change in particular relates directly to our concern with themes. Francis de Sales, in his *Introduction to the Devout Life,* recognized the difficulty the average person has in attempting to "compose the place."[21] The usual tendency was to accomplish this task by means of similitude, i.e., developing images of various elements of the scene based on one's experience of similar objects in one's own environment. De Sales contended that the making of such images can be burdensome to the mind, especially when one's experience is limited. He advocated therefore that one begin with a simple proposal of the *theme* of the event or scene being meditated upon. For example, the theme of meditation on the birth of Christ might be humility, or adoration. The three stages of the meditation process remain, but they are now guided by a clear conception of the theme to which the meditation is directed. Martz concludes that

the enormous popularity of methodical meditation in this era may be attributed to the fact that it satisfied and developed a natural, fundamental tendency of the human mind—a tendency to work from a particular situation, through analysis of that situation, and finally to some sort of resolution of the problems which the situation has presented.[22]

In addition to the development of a thematic dimension to the meditation process, there is another development that also has direct relevance to our concerns here. This is the fact that, in Puritanism, this meditation process was adapted to the personal experience of the meditator. The event need not be an event in the life of Christ or a saint, but might be an event in one's own life. Here again, the process of memory, understanding, and will was retained, but the composition of place could now involve a scene or event in which one was directly involved.

A dramatic example of this process can be cited from early Puritanism. In an autobiographical account published in a collection of sixty-one testimonies under the title *Spirituall Experiences of Sundry Beleevers*, a woman known only as M.K. recounts the following experience.[23] She had been having marriage problems because her husband lived beyond his means, and she barely restrained herself from acting on the temptation to murder him. She felt extremely guilty over this temptation but could not come to any peace about the matter. Then, after eleven years of struggling to rid herself of her sense of guilt, she went to bed one evening and, in the middle of the night, was suddenly awakened by her pet dog who had jumped on the bed. Her immediate reaction was that the devil had come in person to take her away: "I screamed forth aloud, but when I perceived it was the dog, and not the Devill, I began to thinke, *That surely there was a God that had preserved me all this while.*" This thought of God's protection may be considered the first or *memory* stage in the meditation process. While someone else might simply have said, "Oh, it's only the dog," and gone back to sleep, this event prompted M.K. to recall how God had been preserving her since her troubles had begun. This recollection also establishes the basic theme of the meditation process, i.e., *God's preservation of his creatures.*

She wept through the rest of the night, and rising early in the morning she went to the highest room in the house. As she looked out of the window, she sought to catch a glimpse of God. She saw the trees, birds, and sky, and thought to herself:

They could not make themselves, no more then I could make my selfe, and that we must needs have a Maker, and this Maker must

be strong and powerfull; then I fell downe upon my knees crying out
on this manner, O God, if there be a God, shew thy selfe to me a
poore miserable wretch, that am at the point to perish; then I thought
I saw the Lord but with a frowning countenance, hee looked upon
me as if he had said, Thou hast displeased me, and I will not heare
thee, and turning his back went from me, which sight was as a dart
thrust through my soul for the space of halfe an houre, divers
thoughts entred into my heart. . . .[24]

Here we have the second or *understanding* stage of the
meditation process. She reflected on the power of God, his
capacity to preserve the birds and trees and sky, but also reflected on her own miserable condition as one on the verge of
perishing. At this point, God did appear to her but in such an
ambiguous way that it left her still uncertain as to whether he
would preserve her from this time forth or allow her to perish.
Hence, this stage of the meditation concluded with "divers
thoughts" entering her heart.

However, as she rose from her knees, she "resolved to become an earnest suiter to him, and not to do anything more
that should displease him, hoping that he would be intreated
for that which is past." Here is the third or *will* stage of the
process, the decision to be a more earnest suitor to God growing out of the understanding she had just gained regarding her
spiritual condition. God has given her no assurance that he will
preserve her indefinitely, but his appearance to her at least
indicates that he would be responsive to her efforts to secure
his favor toward her. Her resolution, then, is consistent with
the rather ambiguous understanding of God reflected in the
preceeding stage of the process.

In this chapter we will be discussing the structure of the
process of pastoral counseling. We will be focusing on the
process itself, noting correspondences between the meditation
process just outlined and the structure of the pastoral counseling session. Our major concern is to identify the role of the
theme in the counseling process. As our example of M.K.
indicates, the theme is the factor that holds the process together as it moves from identification of event, through mem-

ory, understanding, and will. In view of the importance of the theme, it is noteworthy that the client-centered counseling method, traditionally conceived to be the most structureless form of counseling, reflects this thematic emphasis. Thus, one of Carl Rogers' clients commented on one of her sessions: "A lot of your responses got home with a small shock—particularly the recurrent theme of 'labels' and 'conformity,' and a lot of that you dug out of quite unpromising-looking material."[25] We will not be discussing Rogers' counseling theory here, but the fact that this client noticed how the counselor kept discerning and commenting upon "recurrent themes" indicates that the counseling process may lend itself to the same thematic considerations developed in our earlier chapters.

The psychologist on whom we will rely most in this chapter is Erik Erikson. First we will first discuss his advocacy of a thematic approach to psychotherapy. Then we will take up his identification of the essential elements of the counseling process and show how these elements lend themselves to thematic considerations. Having developed this thematic understanding of the counseling process, we will conclude the chapter with a thematic analysis of an actual pastoral counseling session.

The Thematic Approach to Psychotherapy

One of the distinctive features of Erikson's approach to psychotherapy is his use of the concept of theme in the therapeutic process. He develops this emphasis on theme in his essay "The Nature of Clinical Evidence."[26] Here he describes his therapeutic work with a young man who had recently interrupted his studies for missionary work abroad to enter psychiatric treatment. Erikson points out that, as therapy proceeded, it was possible to discern a "central theme" in the young man's interactions with persons who mattered a great deal to him. Erikson describes the young man's central theme in this way: "Whenever I begin to have faith in somebody's strength and love, some angry and sickly emotions pervade the relationship, and I end up mistrusting, empty, and a victim of anger and despair." This theme deals with the young man's characteristic way of interacting with other persons. In event after event, the young man's initial faith in others degenerates into mistrust, anger, a sense of victimization and despair.

Erikson says that this central theme was the focus of his interpretation of the young man's difficulties to the young man himself. He acknowledges that the words used in such an interpretation "are hard to remember and when reproduced or recorded often sound as arbitrary as any private language developed by two people in the course of an intimate association." But he says that, however worded, an interpretation should express this central, or unitary, theme:

Whatever is said, a therapeutic interpretation, while brief and simple in form, should encompass a *unitary theme* such as I have put before you, a theme common at the same time to a dominant trend in the patient's relation to the therapist, to a significant portion of his symptomatology, to an important conflict of his childhood, and to corresponding facets of his work and love life.[27]

Erikson observes that all this sounds more complicated than it really is: "Often, a very short and casual remark proves to have encompassed all this; and the trends are . . . very closely related to each other in the patient's own struggling mind."

For our purposes here, the important feature of Erikson's discussion of his work with the former seminarian is his emphasis on the unitary theme. The unitary theme that encompasses all of the young man's interactions (including his relationship with his therapist) involves initial faith in another person's strength and love eventually degenerating into mistrust, anger, a sense of victimization and despair. The therapeutic task in this case is to secure a variation on this unitary theme, i.e., an interaction in which the patient's initial faith is sustained, thus initiating a new series of interactions with a considerably different outcome.

Elements of the counseling process. Erikson does not go on to elaborate the basic principles of a thematic approach to psychotherapy. However, in his essay on clinical evidence he does list the elements that are essential parts of any therapeutic process: (1) the *contract* between therapist and patient; (2) the patient's *complaint* of pain or dysfunction; (3) the patient's *symptomatology;* (4) the *reconstruction* of the history of the disturbance; (5) *diagnostic interpretation* of the evidence; and (6) determining the *method of treatment.* In Erikson's judgment, three of these elements are especially important in *psycho*therapeutic work. These include the following elements of the process: complaint (2), reconstruction (4), and diagnostic interpretation (5). In discussing these three elements of the psychotherapeutic process, Erikson pays considerable attention to the thematic nature of couseling. He also cites the use of the Thematic Apperception Test (obviously a thematic device) to assist in clarifying the young man's complaint. Thus, by focusing on the central elements of the psychotherapeutic process, Erikson shows how psychotherapy lends itself to a thematic approach. If this is true of psychotherapy, it can also be shown to be true of the counseling process in pastoral counseling.

Pastoral Counseling as Thematic Process

In the following discussion of the counseling process as it occurs in pastoral counseling, I want to develop a relationship between the traditional meditation structure and the pastoral counseling session. This involves noting correspondences between the stages of the meditation process and the elements of the counseling process. The purpose of noting these correspondences is to show how thematic considerations are not only central to the counseling process but also give the process its essential unity.

1. *Counselee's complaint (Composition of place).* The first phase of the counseling process involves identifying the problem or event that has brought the counselee to the pastor for help. While this phase of the counseling session might seem to be rather preliminary to the counseling itself, it is actually quite integral to the counseling process. The counselee may have as much difficulty articulating the problem as the medita-

tor has in composing the place or seeing the spot toward which the whole meditational process will be directed. The counselee may not have a clear idea of what the problem is. The counselee may bring forward a problem that is not the problem he would want to discuss if he felt free to do so. Or the counselee may lack the necessary experience in verbalizing his problems (similar to the problem of meditating by means of similitude). Clearly, identifying the counselee's problem or complaint is not merely preliminary to the therapeutic process. In fact, his own difficulty in identifying precisely what his problem is, or in talking about the problem once he has indicated what it is, may well become the focus of the counseling session.

One of the most vexing problems confronting the pastoral counselor at this stage of the counseling process is that of determining whether the problem that the counselee has identified as his problem (and as the reason for seeking help) is the "real" problem. There is the counselee who says her problem is her unruly children, when her "real" problem is that she and her husband are on the verge of divorce. There is the parishioner who has a complaint about how the pastor conducts the worship service but whose "real" problem is that he has been informed by his doctor that he has a serious heart condition. The pastoral counseling literature is replete with warnings that, if a parishioner says his problem is one thing, it may well be quite another. The pastor should be especially wary—so says the literature—when the parishioner comes to the pastor with a problem involving the church and its beliefs. The parishioner who wants to talk to the pastor about his doubts concerning life after death has undoubtedly come to talk about another, more urgent problem—e.g., marital difficulties.

A thematic understanding of the complaint stage of the counseling process can help to sort this particular problem out. If the counseling session is thought of as a whole thematic structure, the "apparent" problem mentioned by the counselee at the beginning of the hour is at least thematically related to the "real" problem that surfaces later in the session. If the counselee comes to the pastor with concerns about life after death, these concerns are at least thematically related to the marital difficulties he is having. *How* they are related thematically will depend on the specific counseling session. *That* they are related is an appropriate assumption for the pastor to operate upon, inasmuch as it is based on evidence (largely derived from studies developed by classical Gestalt psychology) that processes have a natural tendency to become assimilated to a principal theme. Thus, rather than clearly differentiating between the "apparent" or "pretended" problem and the "real" problem, the thematic understanding of this stage of the counseling process takes the view that the initial problem as stated by the counselee is thematically related to the deeper or more urgent problem that surfaces later in the counseling session. Counseling proceeds on the basis that the represented problem has thematic continuities with the deeper or more urgent problem that has not yet been articulated. The counselee's representation of his problem is comparable to a Thematic Apperception Test narrative. These narratives may not relate the subject's most compelling problems, and may even go to considerable lengths to disguise them, but the narrative nonetheless manifests thematic continuities with the subject's own problems.

In very practical terms, this means that the counselor need not adopt a suspicious or impatient attitude when the counselee identifies a problem that does not seem to warrant counseling: "Come now, you would not have made a special trip to my office just to talk about Jimmy's trouble with his gym teacher." Instead, the counselor considers the counselee's identification of his problem to be no less than the representation of the problem that he cannot bring himself to talk about at first, if not that problem itself. By taking the stated problem as at least a representation of the deeper problem rather than challenging it, the counselor does not force the counselee to protest: "If you don't think Jimmy's problems with his gym teacher are important, then I will go to someone who does." This understanding of the thematic structure of the counseling session also avoids the situation in which the counselee's words are not taken seriously until his account of the "apparent" or "pretended" problem is concluded and he moves to the "real" problem. If the represented problem is thematically related to the deeper problem, discussion of this represented problem will not be thought of as merely allowing the counselee to get some peripheral concerns off his chest before getting down to the real business of counseling. Instead, this discussion will be seen to be continuous with whatever is to come later in the session. Thus, even if the counselor has reason to suspect that exploration of Jimmy's problems with his gym teacher is a kind of "playing along" with Jimmy's mother, the counselor joins in the play because he can assume that the problem has thematic continuities with the counselee's more serious problems. (Haydn's *Surprise Symphony*, in which a marked thematic discontinuity was introduced to jolt listeners from their slumbers, is the exception that proves the rule.)

2. *Reconstruction of the problem (Memory)*. The second stage of the counseling process explores the various facets of the counselee's problem. This ordinarily involves determining what caused the problem to assume its present form. On the surface, this stage of the process may appear to consist largely of the counselor gathering information from the counselee about the various dimensions of his problem. But as the information gathering proceeds, the counselor begins to identify thematic connections between the various narrative threads of the counselee's story. As Erikson indicates, his therapy sessions with the young former seminarian involved recognizing thematic similarities in the various interpersonal relationships recounted. In identifying these thematic connections, the counselor is particularly attentive to indications of thematic variations. For example, a counselee having professional difficulties may tell the counselor: "All the jobs I have held down have been just plain boring. No challenge whatsoever. There was nothing in any of them that interested me or made me want to work hard." But then the counselee pauses and reflects for a moment: "You know, come to think of it, there was one job that was different from the rest. I wasn't in it very long.

I'd been hired to fill in for someone else when he was on vacation. But I just loved that job. The foreman was helpful; he showed me how to do the job. I looked forward to going to work in the morning and didn't feel tired when I came home in the evening, even though it was tough physical labor." What is behind this variation on the theme of boring jobs? Is there something intrinsic to this job that makes it really different from the rest? And, if so, what is it? Did the counselee enjoy this job because he knew it was not permanent? Or was it because the job foreman treated him respectfully? Or was it the physical labor? Clearly, this variation on the basic theme of professional difficulty merits further exploration. The counselor identifies not only themes but also variations on themes.

This identification of themes and variations on themes in the reconstruction phase of the counseling process gives this phase a coherence it would otherwise lack. While the complaint phase of the process is relatively well focused, the reconstruction phase often lacks direction. As the reconstruction of the problem continues, the counselor sometimes explores all sorts of tangents, amassing considerable information about the problem that has brought the counselee to him, but wondering, as he amasses this data, what it all amounts to. During this reconstruction phase of the counseling process, the counselor is most likely to become impatient with the counselee as the latter seems to get distracted from the major point he wants to make and goes off into various tangents that the counselor suspects will bear little fruit. Also, during this reconstruction phase the counselor is most likely to feel he needs to take a more active role in channeling the process.

A thematic understanding of the counseling process offers a solution, or at least some suggestions that approach a solution, to this problem of the aimlessness of the reconstruction phase. Identification of themes and variation on themes gives the reconstruction phase a sense of direction, even in counseling that is based on "nondirection" principles. The reconstruction phase usually lacks direction because the counselor does not know what to do with the counselee's story once it has been related to him. The counselor allows the narrative to become disjointed and tangential because he does not know how he is to react once the story has been told. He permits the counselee to draw his story out to almost indefinite lengths because he fears the awkward silence that awaits the two of them once the story is told and the counselee awaits his reaction.

Some ministers have met this potentially awkward moment in the counseling session by offering their best advice, recounting their own experiences with a similar problem, or launching into a complex psychological or theological interpretation that puzzles, overwhelms, or threatens the counselee. But other ministers have absorbed enough pastoral counseling theory to realize that these procedures are not highly recommended. Ministers who are bereft of other procedures find themselves continuing to gather more and more tangential information in lieu of a suitable response to the counselee's basic story. Thus, the problem of how to respond to the counselee's story is perhaps most acute for the counselor who "knows" that the appropriate response is not to moralize, to tell a similar story about himself, or to launch immediately into a complex theological or psychological analysis of the story.

The thematic understanding of the reconstruction phase of the counseling process recommends an alternative way of drawing the reconstruction phase toward an appropriate sense of closure. This recommendation involves formulating the themes of the counselee's account and communicating this formulation to him. This communication not only gives evidence to the counselee that his story has been heard and understood, it also provides the counselee an opportunity to modify or even reject the counselor's understanding of the problem. If the counseling session then proceeds to deeper probings into the theological and/or psychological dimensions of the account, there is greater likelihood that the counselee will have confidence in these probings because they have been developed out of an accurate hearing of the story itself.

In short, the reconstruction phase of the counseling process involves the identification of themes as the counselee's story is being told, and it concludes with the counselor communicating these themes to the counselee for his response. As Erikson says concerning the reconstruction stage, the counselor "has no right to test his reconstructions until his trial formulations have combined into a comprehensive interpretation which feels right to him, and which promises, when appropriately verbalized, to feel right to the patient." But once the counselor is reasonably certain of the "rightness" of his understanding of the situation, he "usually finds himself compelled to speak, in order to help the patient in verbalizing his affects and images in a more communicative manner, and to communicate his own impressions." Thus Erikson warns against concluding the listening period too soon in one's concern to verbalize a comprehensive interpretation, but he also suggests that when the reconstruction has proceeded far enough to enable the counselor to verbalize an interpretation with confidence, he needs to proceed with this interpretation and not allow the reconstruction phase to disintegrate into an aimless and pointless quest for more and more details.

3. *Diagnostic interpretation (Understanding).* This brings us to the third or diagnostic interpretation stage of the counseling process. Once the counselor has communicated his identification of the major theme or themes involved in the counselee's narrative, and once the counselee has had a chance to respond to the counselor's formulation of these themes, the process moves to the diagnostic interpretation. This usually involves using the thematic formulation of the problem to generate a diagnostic assessment of the counselee's situation. The themes are placed within a diagnostic framework.

To illustrate how this can work, we may consider John Wesley's visit to Mr. Töltschig, the Moravian pastor, for counseling. As Wesley tells the story, the pastor asked Wesley what the effect of his marriage to Sophy would be on her spiritual condition. When Wesley indicated that it would undoubtedly help her in this regard, the pastor said, "Then I see no reason why you should not marry her." Wesley left the pastor's office deeply perplexed. He evidently expected Pastor Töltschig to advise him differently. While not ruling out the possibility that a diagnostic interpretation might include some advice giving, a diagnostic interpretation of Wesley's problem would undoubtedly focus on the major theme identified in the reconstruction phase of the process, i.e., the theme (or some facet of the theme) of *resignation.* It would draw attention to Wesley's sense of being caught in a forced-choice situation, in that he must choose between Sophy and his ministry because he could not devote himself fully to both. The counselor might suggest, as part of his diagnosis, that they explore the assumptions on which this sense of resignation is based. They could explore the personal motivations that lie behind Wesley's concern about the effect of marriage to Sophy on his career: Is he motivated by a feeling of superiority to Sophy? Is he motivated by doubts concerning her capacity to be a good minister's wife? Or they could focus on some of the psychosocial circumstances that are involved in his spirit of resignation, such as his friends' opposition to the marriage, the pressures exerted by Sophy's uncle and aunt, and the fact that he is her pastor. They could identify untapped personal resources available to Wesley in coping with this forced-choice situation, such as insights gained from previous experiences in which he felt torn between two courses of action. Or perhaps the grounds for this sense of resignation need to be clarified or probed more deeply: Is Wesley simply having misgivings about marriage to this particular young woman, or are there larger conflicts involving his capacity for intimacy with individuals of the opposite sex? Or this sense of resignation may be explored in relation to the deeper intentions of shared human experience: Does he have doubts, on the basis of their relationship thus far, that he and Sophy have an enduring love for each other?

If the counselee is unreceptive to such explorations, the counselor may simply have to proceed to the issue of conflict resolution itself. He may observe that the resolution of the conflict appears to be a matter of much urgency to the counselee, that he would like to respond helpfully to this sense of urgency. This latter suggestion would be based on the fact that, when the resigned individual has come to the resolution that a choice or decision must be made, he often feels a strong sense of urgency about it. This suggestion would enable the two of them to discuss, or make plans to discuss, some of the more immediate questions and problems relating to what the counselee will do in the very near future. These questions and problems may include questions as to what will be the nature of the decision, what problems will be encountered in his communication of his decision to Sophy, what his feelings about this decision are, what he will do when the decision is made about his future, and so on.

Obviously, this is only a hypothetical illustration of a diagnostic interpretation. The important point, however, is that the diagnostic interpretation grows out of the themes identified and agreed upon by counselor and counselee in the reconstruction stage. The diagnostic interpretation is based on these themes but goes beyond them in attempting to diagnose the counselee's current situation in the light of these themes. And notice, too, that the diagnosis ideally includes the counselor's appreciation for the variant forms these themes might take. The diagnosis explores options open to the counselee and invites the counselee to reflect on these options.

Concerning the form that the diagnostic interpretation takes, Erikson points out that he attempts to keep the verbalization of the diagnostic interpretation brief and to the point. In his counseling of the young former seminarian, he renders the unitary theme in diagnostic language by pointing to the way in which the young man placed too much of the burden for his recovery on the counselor and not enough on himself:

I also told him without anger, but not without some honest indignation, that my response to his account had included a feeling of being attacked. I explained that he had worried me, had made me feel pity, had touched me with his memories, and had challenged me to prove, all at once, the goodness of mothers, the immortality of grandfathers, my own perfection, and God's grace.[28]

Thus, in communicating his indignation to the young man, Erikson diagnoses his counselee's unnecessary attempts to burden the counselor with a future that he could himself learn to manage. This comment was not intended "to be a therapeutic 'suggestion' or a clinical slap on the back, but was based on what I knew of his inner resources as well as of the use he made of the opportunities offered in our clinical community." Here, the counselor's diagnosis takes cognizance of the variant forms the young man's basic or unitary theme might take. The young man may continue to experience the inevitable deterioration of his relationships with others by demanding too much of them (as he has demanded too much of the counselor), but the counselor also includes in his diagnosis his considered judgment that the young man has the inner resources necessary to change this usual pattern of interpersonal relationships.

4. *Method of treatment (Will)*. While the three stages of complaint (composition of place), reconstruction (memory), and diagnostic interpretation (understanding) are the heart of the counseling process, this process would not be complete if it were to terminate with the latter. In fact, it is worth noting that, where physical illness or impairment is concerned, the restoration of the health of the patient has only just begun when the diagnostic interpretation has been rendered. In a similar way, the larger part of the counseling task is that of changing the counselee's current condition. In the language we have been employing in this study, this involves securing a variation in the counselee's thematic pattern. Given this therapeutic objective, a fourth and necessary part of the process is what Erikson calls the *method of treatment*. In failing to include this stage among the major stages of the psychotherapeutic process, Erikson did not intend to minimize its importance. Rather, he meant to recognize that the method of treatment grows out of the diagnostic interpretation but need not be confined to the psychotherapeutic process itself. In assessing the future of the young former seminarian, he points out that the young man could be

helped, if hospitalized, by the social influences of the "therapeutic community," and by well-guided work activities—all of which would have to be taken into account, if I were concerned here with the nature of *the therapeutic process* rather than with that of clinical evidence.[29]

In a similar way, the method of treatment that issues from the diagnostic interpretation in the pastoral counseling session may not involve additional counseling. It, too, may focus on external resources of various kinds. In practical terms, this might involve using the resources of the church itself. However, to avoid the assumption that this simply means getting the counselee "involved" or "active" in some facet of the local church's program, the thematic understanding of counseling says that the method of treatment needs to grow directly out of the diagnostic interpretation and therefore reflect the basic themes of the counselee's complaint. Involvement, even in "well-guided work activities," is not a method of treatment unless it is clearly indicated by the counselee's basic themes.

It may also be emphasized that the relationship between the treatment and diagnostic stages is reciprocal. The diagnostic interpretation directly influences the selection of the method of treatment, and the effectiveness of the treatment is evidence of the accuracy of the interpretation. In practical terms, this means that if the problem has been accurately diagnosed, the movement of the counseling process to the treatment stage should flow quite naturally. The counselee will either "know" what needs to be done without any prompting from the counselor, or the pastor and counselee will be able to discuss freely the various options (or thematic variations) that are open to the counselee in the light of the diagnostic interpretation. On the other hand, if the attempt to develop a diagnostic interpretation has failed for one reason or another, there is not much to be gained from attempting to proceed to the treatment stage. Proposals for alleviating the problem (including referral to another professional) will undoubtedly be met with resistance or only passive assent. In this case, the counselor will want to suspend exploration of treatment measures until it is possible for both parties to gain a convincing sense that the problem has been correctly diagnosed. To be sure, the correctness of the diagnostic interpretation does not necessarily depend on the verbal assent of the counselee. The interpretation offered by the counselor may be on target even though the counselee rejects it. But this does not justify moving ahead to the treatment stage on the assumption that the counselee will eventually come to see the correctness of the pastor's interpretation of his problem. Further exploration of the grounds for this rejection is to be preferred to moving ahead to the treatment stage. Is the counselee's rejection of the interpretation only the denial of a truth that he cannot or will not acknowledge? Or has the counselor failed to include in his diagnosis factors that, in the counselee's view, would yield important variations on the central theme?

This discussion of the counselee's assent to or dissent from the diagnostic interpretation assumes, of course, that the counselee's problem can in fact be rightly interpreted. There are various problems that contain too many unknowns to enable the counselor to advance such an interpretation. In these cases, the appropriate move may be to resolve some of these unknowns; another reason, in effect, for suspending the movement of the therapeutic process to the treatment stage. Alternatively, the diagnostic interpretation may include the assessment that the situation, as reconstructed, remains ambiguous and unclear. In this case, any treatment agreed upon by the counselor and counselee will appropriately reflect this very ambiguity. The treatment may be adopted with unusual tentativeness, or it may have an experimental quality to it that both counselor and counselee recognize and support. M.K.'s act of *will* was itself based on a diagnosis of her situation that recognized its fundamental ambiguity.

The treatment stage of the counseling process could be discussed in much greater detail. The foregoing comments, however, indicate that the thematic understanding of the counseling process considers the treatment to be an integral part of the process itself. As indicated, its relationship to the diagnostic stage is a reciprocal one. Expressed in the language of thematic meditation, understanding and will are so closely related that they are mutually corrective of one another. Indeed, all four stages of the process are so integrally related that, together, they constitute a meaningful gestalt. Like the process of meditation, the counseling process as described here reflects, as Martz puts it, "a natural, fundamental tendency of the human mind—a tendency to work from a particular situation, through analysis of that situation, and finally to some sort of resolution of the problems which the situation has presented."[30] Pastoral counseling that intends less than this aborts this natural and fundamental tendency of individuals to resolve their problems.

Unfortunately, in their concern to avoid the obvious errors of a previous generation of pastors, the client-centered pastoral counselors in the 1960's tended to limit their counseling to the first two or, at best, the first three stages of the counseling process. They felt that *understanding* was the culmination of the counseling process, that through understanding one's problem, one can be virtually assured of its rectification. This viewpoint was contested by the reality- or behavior-oriented counselors of the late 1960's and early 1970's, who have tended to limit the counseling process to the first and fourth stages (i.e., complaint and method of treatment). As a corrective of the earlier model, which lacked any serious attention to the component of *will,* behavior-oriented counseling has made a significant contribution. We have been arguing here, however, that *understanding* and *will* are intractably related to one another. A comprehensive theory of pastoral counseling must include all four stages. Significantly, the religious counselors who adopted and refined the techniques of meditation of the sixteenth and seventeenth centuries recognized that complaint (composition of place), reconstruction (memory), diagnostic interpretation (understanding), and method of treatment (will) constitute a thematic whole.

A Case of Premarital Counseling

Thus far, we have discussed the counseling process in rather abstract fashion. I would therefore like to conclude this chapter by illustrating the thematic approach to pastoral counseling. Our illustration is a case of premarital counseling. In considering this case, we will not assess the pastor's counseling skills except insofar as they have direct bearing on the issue of the counseling process and its various stages. The pastor who did the counseling in this case was not attempting to structure the session in terms of the four stages outlined above. The question we will be addressing, therefore, is whether the counseling session would have profited from a more self-conscious employment of this basic structure.

A few words about the situation that brought the young couple to the pastor for premarital counseling: The Cole family are members of Pastor Dickens' church. Mr. and Mrs. Cole have forbidden their eighteen-year-old daughter, Valerie, to visit her fiancé, Bill Jackson (age twenty) in his apartment. Bill shares an apartment with his friend Harry Kirkland. Valerie and Bill accused Mr. and Mrs. Cole of lacking trust in them. There was a heated argument after church one Sunday during which the Coles denied a lack of trust in their daughter. At the conclusion of the argument, Mr. Cole said that Valerie must abide by her parents' wishes or she would have to move out of the house. Faced with this ultimatum, Valerie and Bill decided they would get married as soon as possible. They had already delayed their marriage plans because Mr. and Mrs. Cole had said they did not think the couple was ready to get married yet. A few days following this argument, Valerie phoned Pastor Dickens and asked him if he would perform their wedding within the next week. The following phone conversation ensued:

PASTOR: Aren't you and Bill overreacting to the argument you had with your parents?

VALERIE: No.

PASTOR: What do your parents think about your plans?

VALERIE: They agree and think that this is the best solution, and they would rather see me leave home and married than to just leave and live alone.

PASTOR: I thought you had not planned to marry for another two years.

VALERIE: That was before, but circumstances are different now and we feel we can make it. Will you be able to marry us on Sunday?

PASTOR: Have you had your blood test and received your marriage license?

VALERIE: Yes, tomorrow we will get all of that arranged.

PASTOR: I wonder if you are moving too fast into marriage. Is there a chance that you could postpone it several weeks or months so that we could have some counseling sessions?

VALERIE: No, we already called Bill's parents and they are coming for the wedding.

PASTOR: O.K., I will officiate at your wedding, but before I do I want to have a session with you and Bill. Let's meet for one hour right after Bible study Wednesday evening.

VALERIE: That will be fine. So Bill and I will see you at your office right after Bible study for a one-hour session.

PASTOR: Right. Good-by.

In this brief phone conversation, Valerie made quite clear that the problem, as she saw it, was that she needed to get married as soon as possible and needed Pastor Dickens to perform the ceremony. Pastor Dickens recognized that this was only part of the problem. He felt they were moving too fast and that they could profit from some counseling before marriage. When he met Valerie and Bill for their one session, he tried to get them to see that they were overreacting to the argument with Mr. and Mrs. Cole.

The Counseling Session

Stage 1. Complaint (Composition of Place)

PASTOR: Boy, it is cold out there. How are you two doing?

VALERIE AND BILL: Fine. (Both smile, she giggles a little.)

PASTOR: I am doing fine, too. Valerie, do you remember our telephone conversation?

VALERIE: Yes, you were surprised to hear we were going to get married.

PASTOR: Do you remember my question?

VALERIE: Yes, you asked me if my parents agreed for us to get married and also if we had applied for our marriage license and taken our blood tests.

PASTOR: You remember correctly, but the question I had in mind was my first question. I asked you, "Aren't you and Bill overreacting to the argument you had with your parents?"

VALERIE: Oh. That question. I remember it now, and I answered we were not overreacting.

BILL: We already had this planned much in advance to move up the date for the wedding.

PASTOR: I thought you told me you had postponed it to two years instead of one year.

BILL: That is true, but we changed our minds now that I have a good job to support both of us.

PASTOR: Is there any way that I could convince you to reconsider postponing the wedding for a couple of months or several weeks so that we may have several weeks to counsel?

BILL: No way, we are ready to get married.

PASTOR: Valerie, is that the way you feel about it?

VALERIE: Yes, we are ready and we will not change our mind. Today we got our blood test and we also applied for our license.

Valerie and Bill are clearly persuaded that whatever their problem is, it has been pretty well settled by their decision to get married. Pastor Dickens is convinced that this solution begs many questions and again suggests that some counseling would be helpful to help them sort things out. The young couple reject this suggestion on the grounds that they are already prepared for marriage. This disagreement over the best way to address the problem carries into the second stage of the counseling session:

Stage 2. Reconstruction (Memory)

PASTOR: I would like to get back to the problem that caused you both to promptly decide to get married. Your parents have told me that you wanted to be together at Bill's apartment and it is not that they don't trust you, but you are young and you could be tempted.

VALERIE: I understand their concern but I don't want to get pregnant, I am not that dumb. Besides, I believe that that is to be saved for after marriage. Because if we were to practice that now, what would we have after marriage?

PASTOR: Am I correct in saying that you and your mother agree on the same morals concerning sexual relations?

VALERIE: Yes, we agree. But where we disagree is on the time limit she and Dad want to place on me when it comes to seeing Bill. I am eighteen and I have the right to vote and to be treated as an adult citizen, but my parents are infringing on my rights. My brothers had rights but my parents don't want to allow me any rights.

BILL: Another reason we want to get married is that this way everybody will be happy.

PASTOR: When you say everybody, who is everybody?

BILL: I mean her mom and dad and us. We are the ones involved and the rest have no business in our personal lives.

PASTOR: So you meant to say that you don't care what Valerie's brothers think?

VALERIE: What he means is that we care but they live their lives and we will live ours.

PASTOR: Valerie, you said a while ago that your rights were being infringed. Do you think that when you get married you are going to have more rights than what you have now?

VALERIE: We are not getting married just so I may have my rights, but yes, I will have more rights.

BILL: See, both of us are going to be equal, we will have the same equal rights. I don't believe that stuff about one person having more rights than the other.

PASTOR: Who is going to wash the dishes, wash clothes, vacuum and keep the apartment clean?

BILL: We will all share the work—Valerie, Harry and I. Besides we have a dishwasher and the apartment is easy to keep clean.

VALERIE: I will probably end up doing most of the work. Yes, my mother warned me about the same thing you are saying, but I can handle it and I don't think I will mind.

PASTOR: How will Harry feel about living with you two, and how will you share your expenses so that it will be fair for the three of you?

BILL: Harry has agreed that we can divide the rent into three parts.

VALERIE: You did not tell me that. I don't think it is fair, maybe we can pay a little over the half but not two-thirds.

BILL: You shut up, you don't know what you are talking about.

PASTOR: Bill, I thought you said a while ago that both of you would be equal in rights and in decisions.

BILL: Well, I was just kidding.

VALERIE: No, you weren't (said firmly, yet smiling).

PASTOR: I do not mean to start sermonizing you now, but let me suggest that you remember never to embarrass each other.

VALERIE: I am glad you are telling him that, because he really embarrasses me when he flirts around other girls in my presence.

PASTOR: Bill, I thought you were ready for marriage. Are you sure you are ready to be Valerie's husband and stop shopping around?

BILL: Yeah, I guess.

PASTOR: You guess? You better be ready!

BILL: Yes, I am ready.

This second stage of the counseling process begins with the pastor directing the conversation back to the issue that prompted Valerie and Bill to make hasty marriage plans, i.e., the argument with Valerie's parents over her desire to visit Bill in his apartment. This achieved the pastor's purposes inasmuch as it forced Bill and Valerie to place their decision to get married immediately in the larger context of their conflict with Valerie's parents. As this reconstruction of the conflict with Valerie's parents continued, the pastor identified the theme of *mutual rights*. He noted its importance to Valerie in her relationship to her parents, and this prompted Bill to say that in their married life together they would have equal rights. But Bill's failure to discuss with Valerie the financial arrangements he had worked out with Harry was clear evidence that the *mutual rights* issue would not be solved merely by their act of marriage. In fact, the ensuing argument between Bill and Valerie dramatized the point that Pastor Dickens had wanted to make all along, i.e., that their problems would not be solved simply by getting married and thereby, as Bill put it, "making everybody happy."

While various other themes might have been discerned in this stage of the counseling process, the theme of *mutual rights* proved a useful one in getting the young couple to begin to at least consider the sorts of issues the pastor had in mind when he suggested a few counseling sessions. Significantly, it was when the pastor picked up the theme of *mutual rights* that first Valerie and then Bill began to confess some doubt or uncertainty that they were ready for marriage. Concerning the fact that she would be expected to do most of the housework, Valerie said somewhat doubtfully, "but I can handle it and I don't think I will mind." Confronted with evidence that he is not always concerned for Valerie's rights as his fiancé, Bill said he "guessed" he was ready to be her husband and stop shopping around. The reconstruction stage had clearly identified an area of potential difficulty in their relationship. It had even caused them to express some uncertainty as to their readiness for marriage.

The counseling session continues into the third stage.

Stage 3. Diagnostic Interpretation (Understanding)

PASTOR: As you begin your married life together, I want you to be thinking about some of the things we talked about tonight. I am worried about your financial plans, especially since they involve a third person. I am also concerned that you are not in agreement about your mutual rights. This worries me because this was the main problem Mr. and Mrs. Cole encountered with Valerie's concept of rights.

VALERIE: We will work on those two problems. We know it won't always be easy but we're going to do the best we can.

BILL: That's right.

PASTOR: Let's close with a word of prayer. "Dear Heavenly Father, we ask your blessing on Valerie and Bill as they take this most important step in their lives. We pray for mutual understanding between Valerie and Bill and Mr. and Mrs. Cole. We also pray for your care and protection of Bill's parents as they travel here for the wedding. Amen."

VALERIE: We will call you tomorrow and talk to you about the ceremony at my house.

PASTOR: All right. I'll expect your call tomorrow. Good night.

This third stage, much shorter than the reconstruction stage, includes an effort by the pastor to diagnose Valerie's and Bill's situation as they anticipate their marriage. His brief diagnostic interpretation is based on the theme discerned in the reconstruction stage of the session, i.e., *mutual rights*. What is not noted in his diagnostic interpretation is the effect that their conversation about mutual rights had on both of them, that it caused them to waver somewhat in their confidence in their readiness for marriage. Had the pastor attempted to formulate this aspect of his diagnosis, it might have been possible to explore the question of their readiness further. Valerie especially seemed willing to open up this issue as the session came to a close. The pastor might encourage the couple to see this problem of readiness for marriage as a constituent part of the mutual rights question. Each has the *right* to expect from the other some careful reflection on his or her readiness for marriage. The pastor might therefore urge a second counseling session within the next few days in which they would explore this issue of readiness for marriage in greater depth. While his earlier proposals for counseling sessions had been rebuffed, this proposal would not be a general recommendation of counseling but a specific suggestion based on the doubts that had begun to surface in tonight's session. Also, by suggesting that it take place within the next few days it would not be presented, as were the earlier proposals for counseling, as merely a means to postpone the couple's marriage plans.

Stage 4. Method of Treatment (Will)

The suggestion of a second counseling session would grow directly out of the diagnostic interpretation itself, and would therefore carry the process into the fourth stage, the method of treatment stage. As it stands, the counseling session does not include the fourth stage of the counseling process. This is partly because the pastor had already agreed to perform the wedding and does not believe he can renege on this promise. Thus, the treatment stage has already been anticipated by the pastor's prior agreement to perform the wedding. Going ahead with the ceremony is the only longer-term option available.

However, this is only one part of the reason that the counseling session does not issue in consideration of a method of treatment. Another part of the reason relates to the fact that the pastor does not extend the question of *mutual rights* to include his own role in the situation. While Valerie and Bill have been concerned about infringements on their own rights, they have not been as responsive to the rights of others. The pastor addressed this problem mainly by reflecting the viewpoint of Valerie's parents. But he has more direct evidence of Valerie and Bill's tendency to neglect their responsibilities for the rights of others in their handling of arrangements for the wedding itself. In making their marriage plans (including arranging for Bill's parents to come for the event) before any consultation with the pastor, they have tended to see him as a necessary means toward a desired end. On the other hand, he has reinforced this tendency by proposing counseling sessions in such a diffident manner as to imply that they would probably not be very useful anyway. Nonetheless, there is a thematic relationship between the conflict with Valerie's parents that initiated the couple's hasty wedding plans and their subsequent interaction with the pastor. While greater concern for the *rights* of the pastor would not be a precondition for his performance of the wedding, this dimension of the *mutual rights* issue is at least partly responsible for the fact that no significant method of treatment could be agreed upon and implemented.

Finally, in discussing this premarital counseling case in terms of the various stages of the counseling process, we have focused primarily on the process itself and have not attempted to evaluate the counselor's overall performance. However, there are some clear indications that his counseling of the couple would have profited from a more self-conscious employment of the basic counseling structure outlined in this chapter. Because the session consisted largely of the first two stages of the process, the relationship between the pastor's role in counseling the couple and his performance of the marriage ceremony remains ambiguous. Had the latter act evolved naturally out of the counseling session, as the preferred "method of treatment," the pastor would undoubtedly have come away with greater confidence in the integral relationship between his pastoral counseling and his formal pastoral acts.

Conclusion

Obviously, a more self-conscious employment of these four stages in the counseling process will not solve all the problems confronted by the pastoral counselor. What we have shown here, however, is that attention to the form or structure of the counseling process will have significant influence on the way the counseling session itself is structured. And, in focusing on the thematic continuity within this structure, the pastoral counselor employs a method that was originally intended to make the devout life more accessible to the ordinary believer.

4

Theological Themes
in Pastoral Counseling

WITH THIS CHAPTER, our study shifts from a predominantly psychological focus to a predominantly theological one. We continue to address the thematic features of pastoral counseling, but we place them in a pastoral theological context.

Over the years, pastoral counseling has become the paradigmatic pastoral function on which both pastoral psychology and pastoral theology have been based. So our discussion of pastoral counseling serves as an appropriate bridge between these two models of pastoral care. Theological issues arise as we address the verbal content of counseling in the pastoral setting. While the *structure* of the counseling process has theological implications, the central theological issues raised in pastoral counseling relate to the *verbal content* of the counseling session. In this chapter, therefore, we will center our attention on the verbal communications that occur in the counseling process. We will be asking: What role can theological understandings play in the thematizing that occurs in pastoral counseling?

Theological Themes

In *The Minister as Diagnostician,* Paul W. Pruyser encourages the pastor to use theological perspectives in his work. He argues that ministers have substituted a psychological for a theological perspective in their pastoral activities. In the area of counseling, this has meant depriving the counselee of the insights and resources that he expected to be employed when he sought the assistance of a minister instead of another professional. To honor the counselee's expectations in this regard, Pruyser recommends the use of "theological themes" in the counseling setting and offers seven such themes: awareness of the holy, providence, faith, grace or gratefulness, repentance, communion, and vocation.

Pruyser does not assume that this is an exhaustive list of theological themes, and he cautions against the temptation to reify these themes, to treat them like psychiatric labels. Rather, the themes

should linger in the pastor's mind, functioning as guideposts to his diagnostic thinking and as ordering principles for the observations he makes. To a lesser degree, they may alert him to dimensions of experience that thus far have not come to the fore, and which may have to be singled out for discussion. In every diagnostic process there is a selective attention as well as selective inattention.[31]

Pruyser says that he offers these warnings against the reification of the theological themes because "something of this sort has happened to Erikson's *identity, doubt, trust, shame,* etc." In the same way that Erikson's psychosocial themes have often been viewed as age-specific personality traits instead of perennial themes, there is always the danger that these theological themes might also be used in a literalistic fashion, i.e., as means to neatly categorize the counselee's experiences.

The meanings of the seven themes may be summarized as follows:

1. *Awareness of the holy.* What is sacred to this individual? Is there anything he regards as untouchable or inscrutable? Does he present himself as one who is ultimately dependent on a power or force beyond himself, or is he greatly self-inflated and prepossessed with himself? Is there a dry, unemotional factualness in his account that shies away from any mystery and rules out anything transcendent?

2. *Providence.* Does the counselee perceive a divine purpose in his life? Does he believe that his world is ultimately benevolent? Does he have a sense of basic trust in the world? Or does

he lack such trust? Is he suspicious of divine promises? Does he believe that reliance on divine guidance implies a deficiency in personal competence?

3. *Faith.* Is the counselee's attitude toward life affirming or negating? Does he experience his religious faith as enlarging (i.e., activating talents, stimulating curiosity, widening his scope of engagements), or as binding and constricting?

4. *Grace or gratefulness.* Can the counselee accept kindness, generosity and acceptance, or does he insist on the finality of his own self-rejection?

5. *Repentance.* Does the counselee have an awareness of himself as an agent in the problems he faces? Does he shoulder appropriate responsibility for his situation? Is he able to experience remorse, regret, sorrow?

6. *Communion.* Does the counselee feel embedded in the groups with which he interacts (family, work associates, friends, fellow religionists)? Or is he estranged or alienated from one or another of these sources of community?

7. *Vocation.* Is the counselee a cheerful participant in the scheme of creation and providence, such that he has a sense of purpose and dedication? Does he have a sense of personal competence and effectiveness? Or does he experience his life as binding, stagnant, and without much future?

To illustrate the potential value of these theological themes for pastoral counseling, Pruyser provides five brief cases in which these themes were used by clergymen. In one case, a male college student named Lambert came to the minister of a church located near the campus and proceeded to relate how his girl friend had dropped him for an older student. Prior to this rejection, he had felt some guilt over his sexual intimacies with the girl, but now these guilt feelings were increased by her rejection of him. As long as there was reason to believe their relationship would be permanent, he did not feel especially guilty about these intimacies.

As the minister listened to Lambert identify his problem and reconstruct its history, he perceived that the young man was genuinely remorseful for his prior actions, but that this remorse was only part of a larger sense of having been abandoned by God. Thus, the pastor reports:

In view of Lambert's nascent sense of sin and repentance it seemed less appropriate to remind him explicitly of God's forgiving grace than to assure him of God's loving providential care for the whole of his life. He picked this up by dwelling on the positive elements of his friendship with the girl, as if to contrast his feeling of uncleanliness with feelings of gratitude.[32]

Thus, the pastor sees *providence* as the primary theological theme in the young man's problem and *repentance* as a relevant but subordinate theme. He also mentions the *communion* theme, observing that "while Lambert's faith is rather privatistic," in coming to the pastor he acted on "some longing to restore a bond with other believers."

This brief example of the use of theological themes in pastoral counseling shows how these themes can be teased out of a counselee's reconstruction of his problem and then used to diagnose it. This example also shows that the themes do not operate in isolation from one another, but rather tend to form patterns through the clustering of two or more prominent themes. The themes of repentance, providence, and communion are all relevant to Lambert's problem, and in related ways.

Theological themes and the counseling process. It is not difficult to see how theological themes can be used in the counseling process as discussed earlier. In effect, Pruyser himself notes that these themes may play a prominent role in the reconstruction and diagnostic stages of the process when he points out that the themes "should linger in the pastor's mind, functioning as guideposts to his diagnostic thinking and as ordering principles for the observations he makes." As ordering principles for reconstruction and guideposts for diagnostic thinking, theological themes are not simply forced on the counselee's narrative. Rather, the counselor discerns their implicit presence in the things the counselee says and how he says them. In Erikson's valuable phrase, he engages in "disciplined subjectivity."[33] He does not proceed in the purely objective fashion of waiting for the counselee to make explicitly theological statements, but neither does he take the purely subjective approach of imputing theological themes to the materials regardless of their verbal content. Instead, he works between these two extremes, using theological themes as principles for ordering his own thoughts about the problem as reconstructed and as guideposts for making diagnostic interpretations. The theological themes are employed in a discriminating way in the pastor's clarification and assessment of the counselee's situation.

But is this the only function of the theological themes? Is their only purpose to assist the pastor himself in understanding the problem? Or are they also involved in communicating these clarifications and assessments to the counselee? As we have seen, Erikson uses psychological themes not only to clarify the problem for himself but also to communicate his understanding of the problem to the counselee. Pruyser does not specifically propose communicating theological themes directly to the counselee. The reason he does not propose this, however, is that this invites various abuses. Explicit use of theological language may, for example, invite sermonizing rather than diagnosis. On the other hand, nothing that Pruyser says in his proposal would necessarily preclude the use of theological themes in communicating with the counselee if this is done properly. The minister who provided most of the cases in Pruyser's book not only used the themes to help him reconstruct and diagnose each situation, he also employed them in communicating his reconstruction and diagnosis to the parishioner concerned. And, if these cases are an indication of how counselees can be expected to respond to this explicit use of theological themes in the communication of the diagnostic interpretation to the counselee, it is noteworthy that these particular counselees did not seem to find this procedure disturbing, puzzling, manipulative, or even particularly unusual. While the diagnostic interpretation in the Lambert case could have been formulated in more psychological language, the fact that Lambert himself contributed supporting evidence for this theologically stated interpretation, and that this part of the discussion had a calming effect on him, is an indication that the theological themes need not always be translated into other forms of discourse. They can sometimes speak for themselves.

Theological and psychosocial themes. On the other hand, this does raise the question of the relationship between psychological and theological themes. The theological themes that Pruyser has selected here have a direct affinity with personal dynamics. Awareness of the holy relates to the counselee's sense of dependence; providence relates to his sense of trust; faith relates to his attitudes toward self-expansion and growth; and so on. Pruyser's rationale for this selection of themes that are related to these personal dynamics is that there is an isomorphism between one's interpersonal relationships and his relationships with the ultimate reality of which theology speaks. Thus, it is not a question in pastoral counseling of having to choose between psychological and theological themes, but of recognizing the relationship between psychological and theological themes. In recognizing this relationship the pastor can explore their complementary uses.

More specifically we can note how Pruyser's theological themes relate to Erikson's psychosocial themes. The diagram on the next page suggests how they might be related. It correlates Pruyser's theological themes and Erikson's psychosocial themes. For purposes of comparing Pruyser's themes with Erikson's schedule of virtues, the virtues are listed adjacent to their corresponding psychosocial themes.

The diagram indicates the following relationships between theological themes and psychosocial themes:

1. *Providence—trust vs. mistrust.* The theological theme focuses on the counselee's sense that the world is under God's guidance and therefore trustworthy. The psychosocial theme concerns the counselee's sense of being able to rely on the sameness and continuity of other providers.

2. *Grace or gratefulness—autonomy vs. shame and self-doubt.* The theological theme recognizes that the counselee often rejects the kindness and generosity of others because he

CORRELATION OF THEOLOGICAL AND PSYCHOSOCIAL THEMES

Theological Themes	Psychosocial Themes	Human Virtues
(1) Providence	Trust vs. Mistrust	HOPE
(2) Grace or Gratefulness	Autonomy vs. Shame and Self-Doubt	WILL
(3) Repentance	Initiative vs. Guilt	PURPOSE
(4) Vocation	Industry vs. Inferiority	COMPETENCE
(5) Faith	Identity vs. Identity Diffusion	FIDELITY
(6) Communion	Intimacy vs. Isolation	LOVE
(7) Vocation	Generativity vs. Stagnation	CARE
(8) Awareness of the Holy	Integrity vs. Despair	WISDOM

has an excessive sense of his own unworthiness. The psychological theme focuses on the counselee's capacity to appropriate the goodwill of others when he is not overcome with feelings of shame and self-doubt.

3. *Repentance—initiative vs. guilt.* The theological theme focuses on the counselee's acceptance of an appropriate level of moral responsibility for his situation. The psychosocial theme focuses on the counselee's capacity not to allow himself to become immobilized by guilt on the one hand or to display excessive self-righteousness on the other.

4. *Vocation—industry vs. inferiority.* The theological theme focuses on the counselee's sense of purpose, dedication, per-

sonal competence, and effectiveness. The psychosocial theme centers on the counselee's capacity to participate in a productive situation and bring it to completion.

5. *Faith—identity vs. identity diffusion.* The theological theme focuses on the counselee's affirmative attitude toward life; his experience of his religious proclivities as widening his scope of engagement. The psychosocial theme centers on the counselee's desire to affirm and be affirmed by others; it manifests itself in a concern to integrate one's experiences to date into a widening radius of psychosocial commitments and expressions of fidelity.

6. *Communion—intimacy vs. isolation.* The theological theme focuses on the counselee's sense of being accepted into the social groups that matter to him. The psychosocial theme focuses on the counselee's capacity to commit himself to concrete affiliations, even though they may call for significant sacrifices and compromises.

7. *Vocation—generativity vs. stagnation.* The theological theme focuses on the counselee's sense of purpose, dedication, personal competence, and effectiveness. The psychosocial theme centers on the counselee's capacity to play a productive role in behalf of other people, especially the younger generation.

8. *Awareness of the holy—integrity vs. despair.* The theological theme focuses on the counselee's relationship to powers or forces beyond himself. The psychosocial theme centers on his sense of comradeship with the cultural forces that have shaped his life.

These points of contact between Erikson's psychosocial themes and Pruyser's theological themes indicate that the pastoral counselor does not need to decide between psychosocial and theological themes. He may appropriately use a combination of psychosocial and theological themes, depending on the circumstances. This is not, however, a mere eclecticism. Their formal relationship and their substantive similarities ensures against the sorts of eclecticisms that result from fusing two or more psychotherapeutic theories. Depending on the needs and interests of the counselee, the counselor may choose to use theological themes, psychosocial themes, or a combination of the two. While this may result in conceptual impurity, it is important to keep in mind that the counselor's objective is not conceptual purity but providing pastoral assistance to people in need.

To indicate how Erikson's psychosocial themes may be employed in this way, we may refer back to the case of Lambert. If the pastor were to communicate his diagnosis in psychosocial rather than theological themes, he would focus on the theme of *trust vs. mistrust* as his dominant theme, i.e., the counselee's current sense of not being able to rely on other individuals (especially, of course, his girl friend). A major subtheme would be the theme of *initiative vs. guilt*, i.e., the counselee's capacity not to allow himself to become immobilized by guilt on the one hand or display excessive self-righteousness on the other. And, finally, a third theme of importance would be the theme of *intimacy vs. isolation*, i.e., the counselee's capacity to commit himself to concrete affiliations that may require sacrifice and compromise. Those three themes correspond to the three theological themes the original counselor developed in his diagnosis of Lambert's problem.

A Case of Bereavement Counseling

Thus far, our only opportunity to see how theological themes may be applied to an individual life in the context of counseling has been our very brief comments about Lambert. I would therefore like to look at the life of another individual in greater depth to see how we might use these theological themes in a diagnostic way. The life I have chosen for this is that of Jeanne Marie Guyon, the seventeenth-century French mystic. Our source is her autobiographical account of her life, written in response to her spiritual director's request for an account of her earlier life.[34] This account was intended to enable her spiritual director—her pastor—to diagnose her situation. And, as she herself pointed out, every effort was made to give full details of her life, no matter how painful, because he had "forbidden me to omit anything" and "had absolutely commanded me to explain everything, and give all particulars." The selection from her autobiography chosen for discussion here is her account of her married life from the time of her marriage until the death of her husband. Given the fact that this account culminates with her husband's death, we may justifiably think of Jeanne as a young widow who has sought pastoral counseling because she is having difficulty getting over her husband's death. This account, which begins with her marriage at age sixteen to a man twenty-two years her senior may be thought of as the complaint and reconstruction phases of the counseling session.

Marriage to a wealthy gentleman. There was a person who had sought me in marriage for some years, whom my father for family reasons had always refused. His manners were a little distasteful to my vanity, yet the fear they had I should leave the country, and the great wealth of this gentleman, led my father, in spite of all his own objections and those of my mother, to accept him for me. It was done without my being told, on the vigil of St. Francis de Sales, 28th January, 1664, and they even made me sign the articles of marriage without telling me what they were. Although I was well pleased to be married, because I imagined thereby I should have full liberty, and that I should be delivered from the ill-treatment of my mother, which doubtless I brought on myself by want of docility, God had quite other views, and the state in which I found myself afterwards frustrated my hopes, as I shall hereafter tell. Although I was well pleased to be married, I nevertheless continued all the time of my engagement, and even long after my marriage, in extreme confusion. . . . The joy at this marriage was universal in our town, and in this rejoicing I was the only person sad. I could neither laugh like the others, nor even eat, so oppressed was my heart. I knew not the cause of my sadness; but it was as if a presentiment God was giving me of what should befall me. Hardly was I married when the recollection of my desire to be a nun came to overwhelm me. All those who came to compliment me the day after my marriage could not help rallying me because I wept bitterly, and I said to them, "Alas! I had once so desired to be a nun; why am I then now married? and by what fatality is this happened to me?"

Mother-in-law problems. I was no sooner at home with my new husband than I clearly saw it would be for me a house of sorrow. I was obliged to change my conduct, for their manner of living was very different from that in my father's house. My mother-in-law, who had been long time a widow, thought only of saving, while in my father's house we lived in an exceedingly noble manner. Everything was showy and everything on a liberal scale, and all my husband and my mother-in-law called extravagance, and I called respectability, was observed there. I was very much surprised at this change, and the more so as my vanity would rather have increased than cut down expenditure. I was more than fifteen years—in my sixteenth year—when I was married. My astonishment greatly increased when I saw I must give up what I had with so much trouble acquired. At my father's house we had to live with much refinement, learn to speak correctly. All I said was there applauded and made much of. Here I was not listened to, except to be contradicted and to be blamed. If I spoke well, they said it was to read them a lesson. If anyone came and a subject was under discussion, while my father used to make me speak, here, if I wished to express my opinion, they said it was to dispute, and they ignominiously silenced me, and from morning to night they chided me. They led my husband to do the same, and he was only too well disposed for it. . . . But we must regard all things in God, who permitted these things for my salvation, and because he would not destroy me. I had, besides, so much pride that if a different conduct had been observed with me, I would have been upheld in that, and I should not, perhaps, have turned to God, as I did eventually, through the wretchedness to which I was reduced by crosses.

To return to my subject, I will say that my mother-in-law conceived such a hostility to me, that in order to annoy me she made me do the most humiliating things; for her temper was so extraordinary, from not having conquered it in her youth, that she could not live with any one. . . . Her whole occupation was to continually thwart me, and she inspired her son with the same sentiments. They insisted that persons far below me should take precedence, in order to annoy me. My mother, who was very sensitive on the point of honor, could not endure this, and when she learned it from others—for I never said anything of it—she found fault with me, thinking I did it from not knowing how to maintain my rank, that I had no spirit, and a thousand other things of this kind. I dared not tell her how I was situated, but I was dying of vexation, and what increased it still more was the recollection of the persons who had sought me in marriage, the difference of their temper and their manner of acting, the love and esteem they had for me, and their gentleness and politeness: this was very hard for me to bear. My mother-in-law incessantly spoke to me disparagingly of my father and my mother, and I never went to see them but I had to endure this disagreeable talk on my return. On the other hand, my mother complained of me that I did not see her often enough. She said I did not love her, that I attached myself too much to my husband; thus I had much to suffer from all sides. What increased still more my crosses was that my mother related to my mother-in-law the troubles I had given her in my childhood, so that the moment I spoke, they reproached me with this, and told me I was a wicked character. My husband wished me to remain all day in the room of my mother-in-law, without being allowed to go to my apartment: I had not therefore a moment for seclusion or breathing a little. She spoke disparagingly of me to every one, hoping thereby to diminish the esteem and affection each had for me, so that she put insults upon me in the presence of the best society. . . .

Caring for sick husband. Such was my married life, rather that of a slave than of a free person. To increase my disgrace, it was discovered, four months after my marriage, that my husband was gouty. This disease, which doubtless has sanctified him, caused me many real crosses both without and within. That year he twice had the gout six weeks at a time, and it again seized him shortly after, much more severely. At last he became so indisposed that he did not leave his room, nor often even his bed, which he ordinarily kept many months. I watched him with great care, and, though I was very young, I did not fail in my duty. I even did it to excess. . . . My own friends used to say that I was indeed of a nice age to be nurse to a sick man; that it was a disgraceful thing not to make use of my talents. . . . Besides, my mother could hardly suffer the assiduity I exhibited to my husband, assuring me I was thereby securing unhappiness for myself, and in the end he would exact as a duty what I was doing as virtue; instead of pitying me, she often found fault with me. It is true that, to look at things humanly, it was a folly to make a slave of myself in this way for persons who had no gratitude for it; but how different were my thoughts from those of all these persons. . . . God made use of all these things for my salvation. Through his goodness he has so managed things that I have afterwards seen this course was absolutely necessary for me, in order to make me die to my vain and haughty natural character. I should not have had the strength to destroy it myself, if God had not worked for it by an altogether wise dispensation of his providence. I urgently asked patience from God. . . .

Husband's death. My husband's ailment became every day more obstinate and he himself had a presentiment of death. His mind was made up for it, for the languishing life he led became every day more burdensome to him. To his other ailments was added a disgust for all kinds of nourishment, so great that he did not even take the things necessary for life. The little he took, there was no one but I had the courage to force on him. . . . I was well prepared for anything it might please Providence to ordain; for I saw some time back he could hardly live longer. His patience increased with his illness, and his illness was very crucifying for me; yet the good use he made of it softened all my troubles. I was extremely pained that my mother-in-law kept me away from his bedside as much as she could, and influenced him against me. I much feared he might die in the feeling, and it afflicted me extremely. I seized a moment, when my mother-in-law was not there, and approaching his bed, I knelt down and said to him, that if I had done anything which had displeased him, I asked his pardon. I begged him to believe it was not voluntarily. He appeared much touched, and as if he had recovered from a profound stupor, he said to me—what he had never said before—"It is I who ask your pardon. I did not deserve you." From this time not only had he no longer a dislike to see me, but he gave me advice as to what I should do after his death, in order not to be dependent on the persons on whom I am at present. He was eight days very resigned and patient; although, owing to the gangrene which increased, they cut him up with a lancet, I sent to Paris to fetch the best surgeon, but he was dead when he arrived.

The period of mourning. As soon as I learned my husband had expired, I said, "O my God, you have broken my bonds. I will offer to you a sacrifice of praise." After that I remained in a very great silence, exterior and interior; silence, however, dry and without support. I could neither weep nor speak. My mother-in-law said very beautiful things, at which every one was edified, and they were scandalized at my silence, which was put down to want of resignation. A monk told me that every one admired the beautiful behavior of my mother-in-law; that as for me, they did not hear me say anything— that I must offer my loss to God. But it was impossible for me to say

a single word, whatever effort I made. I was, besides, much pros-
trated, for although I had recently given birth to my daughter, I
nevertheless watched my husband without leaving his room the
twenty-four nights he was ill. I was more than a year in recovering
from the fatigue of that. The prostration of body and the prostration
of my spirit, the dryness and stupidity I was in, made me unable to
speak. . . . I saw that crosses would not be wanting to me since my
mother-in-law had survived my husband; and I could not understand
God's conduct, which, while setting me free, had yet more strongly
bound me by giving me two children immediately before the death
of my husband. This surprised me extremely, that God set me at
liberty only by making me captive. I have since learned that he had
by his wisdom provided for me a means of being afterwards the
plaything of his providence. . . .

Theological diagnosis of Jeanne Marie Guyon. When this
"counseling session" begins, it might appear that Jeanne
Guyon is denying the reality of her husband's death by focusing on the circumstances of their marriage. But, as the session
continues, it becomes clear that these circumstances are directly related to her husband's death and its effect on her life.
Why she married Jacques Guyon and what effect her husband's death is having on her life are thematically related; it
would not have been appropriate for the counselor to interrupt
the counselee's recital of her marriage to Jacques Guyon by
saying, "But that's all in the past; the real reason you came to
see me is that your husband's death leaves you uncertain about
your future." The two problems are thematically related, and
Jeanne herself knows that her husband's death needs to be
understood within the context of these earlier marital problems. What occurs throughout most of the account, therefore,
is a reconstruction of the problem. As Jeanne takes responsibility for developing this reconstruction, the "counselor" is discerning the themes that hold this account together and give
it coherence. What are these themes? If we were Jeanne's
counselor, what would we communicate to her? How would we
formulate this reconstruction thematically? And how would we
diagnose her current situation in thematic terms?

Among Pruyser's seven themes, the dominant theme in this account is *providence*. As indicated earlier, this theme of providence focuses on the following concerns: Does the counselee perceive a divine purpose in his life? Does he believe that his world is ultimately benevolent? Does he have a sense of basic trust in the world? Or does he lack such trust? Is he suspicious of divine promises? Does he believe that reliance on divine guidance implies a deficiency in personal competence? Concerns about providence are a recurring theme throughout this selection. For example, at the very beginning of the account, Jeanne points out that God protected her from spiritual ruin by not permitting her to marry individuals that pleased her: "I was sought for by many persons who seemed good matches for me; but God, who would not consent to my ruin, did not permit such things to succeed." Later, she saw that her problems with her mother-in-law were actually evidences of God's concern for her: "But we must regard all things in God, who permitted these things for my salvation, and because he would not destroy me." Then, when her husband became sick and later died, she uses the very language of providence to describe these events: "The first few days he was there he appeared to be better, when suddenly he was seized by a colic and continued fever. I was well prepared for anything it might please Providence to ordain; for I saw some time back he could hardly live longer." Similarly, after his death, she reflected on her future in terms of God's providence: "This surprised me extremely, that God set me at liberty only by making me captive. I have since learned that he had by his wisdom provided for me a means of being afterwards the plaything of his providence."

These statements about providence suggest that Jeanne Guyon strongly perceives a divine purpose in her life. God regularly intervenes in her life and protects her from the mistakes she would have made had he not been there to guide her. On the other hand, her account also reflects some uncertainty as to whether this divine purpose is always benevolent and worthy of her trust. She has suspicions that God's actions are not in her best interests, but she pushes these suspicions aside, saying that his purposes were beyond her understanding at the time. Note, too, that she does not totally reject her own capacity to discern what the future holds. She says that she was prepared for her husband's death not only because she accepted whatever God had in store for her but also because she could see for herself that he was dying. Thus, she does not claim to influence events, but she does affirm her capacity (with God's help) to make her own judgments and observations about these events.

This strong focus on the theme of providence is coupled with an especially negative experience of *communion.* As indicated earlier, this theme asks: Does the counselee feel embedded in the groups with which he or she is related? Or is the counselee estranged or alienated from one or another of these sources of community? Negative statements about Jeanne's family life abound. Her family relationships are binding and constricting. Her role not only as daughter-in-law and wife, but also as mother, is confining. On the other hand. she provides an image of what a positive and supportive community would be for her when she recalls her earlier upbringing: "At my father's house we had to live with much refinement, learn to speak correctly. All I said was there applauded and made much of." Here we have a variation on the negative communion theme. A satisfying community would be one in which she was more at the center of attention. In her husband's home, her mother-in-law was the central figure. Thus, communion is a negative theme for her, but at the same time she expresses a positive variation on this theme, indicating how this problem of communion could perhaps be alleviated.

The theme of *repentance* is also important in this account. As indicated, this theme is concerned with the following issues: Does the counselee have an awareness of being an agent in the problems he or she faces? Is the counselee shouldering appropriate responsibility for the situation, and also able to experience remorse, regret, sorrow? Many of Jeanne's comments on this theme assign blame to other people for her situation. Her own mother thinks her problems are largely her own fault: "She found fault with me, thinking I did it from not knowing how to maintain my rank, that I had no spirit, and a thousand other things of this kind." But Jeanne contends that her husband and his mother are largely to blame: "I have had large experience of crosses, but I have never found any more difficult to bear than that of an unrelaxing contrariety, and while one does what one can to satisfy persons, in place of succeeding, to offend by the very things that ought to oblige them." There are many statements of this kind in the account, in which she blames other people for her circumstances. But does she assume any personal responsibility for the situation she is in? Does she shoulder any blame herself? There are some instances of this, but because they typically occur in the context of her accusations against other people, they are rather muted. Thus, Jeanne comments on the ill-treatment she received from her own mother, which, she says, "doubtless I brought on myself by want of docility." Also, in the deathbed confession episode, she knelt down beside her husband and said to him "that if I had done anything which had displeased him, I asked his pardon." It is noteworthy that her confession is stated in conditional language, and is unspecific ("*if* I had done anything"). Is this a genuine confession of guilt on her part? Or is it primarily designed to evoke a confession from him?

Other theological themes are represented in this account. Her *awareness of the holy* is reflected in her view that God's purposes are often inscrutable. On the other hand, her sense of *faith* is largely binding and constricting. She does not feel that God supports her desire for autonomy and for opportunities of self-expression. On the contrary, he wants to bind and constrict her lest she become overly independent, prideful, and vain. With regard to *grace*, she does not sense herself to be the recipient of kindness and generosity. While her marriage actually meant relinquishing much of the lavishness of her father's home, she says that she had actually hoped for a situation even more lavish than she had known as a child. On the other hand, her sense of not being the recipient of kindness and generosity is not based on a self-rejecting attitude, a feeling that she is unworthy of grace, but solely on the fact that her husband and mother-in-law were not generous people. And, finally, *vocation* is conspicuous by its absence. Her life under the present circumstances lacks purpose and dedication; it affords no opportunities for personal competence and effectiveness; the future appears limited. At the same time, there are strong indications that a sense of vocation, under other communal circumstances, would be a major positive factor in her life. If, during her earlier childhood, she enjoyed being at the center of attention, this was not only because she wanted to be admired for her physical qualities but also because she enjoyed demonstrating her abilities and competence.

To summarize the foregoing assessment of Jeanne Guyon's theological themes, the theme of *providence* is the dominant theological theme, and *communion* and *repentance* are the major subthemes. Because these two subthemes are largely expressed in negative terms, this influences her toward a less mature understanding of providence than might otherwise have been the case. She does not feel that present communal relations justify a more trusting view toward the world, and she cannot acknowledge much personal responsibility for her current situation.

The other themes largely reinforce the three major themes. Her *awareness of the holy* reinforces her view that providence is inscrutable at times, and her sense of *faith* and *grace* reflect her negative experience of communion and repentance. The puzzling feature of this thematic pattern is the theme of *vocation* which, as we have said, is conspicuous by its absence. If vocation were present, would it express a variation on the major themes expressed here? How would the whole thematic pattern be changed if she had an opportunity to participate in God's purposes rather than view herself as merely the "plaything of his providence"? How would the whole pattern be different if she could realistically envision demonstrating her abilities to a group of admirers and experience herself as an actor and not as merely the victim of other people's actions?

How might the counselor express this thematic pattern in a diagnostic interpretation of Jeanne Guyon's current situation? A diagnostic interpretation that would be faithful to the foregoing reconstruction might consist of two parts. First, there would be the basic theme, e.g.: "You continually emphasize that God has definite purposes for your life. But you also indicate that his purposes often frustrate your hopes. There is a conflict between what you believe God wants for you and what you want for yourself." This statement of the basic theme could be followed up with an example: "This conflict is especially evident in your relations with other people. You indicate that God wants you to be subjected to the contrariness of other people, but you also seem at times to resist this subjection to other people and to resist this understanding of God and his purposes for you." Second, there is a variation on this basic theme, e.g.: "Your sense of conflict between what God wants for you and what you want for yourself does not appear to you to be an unresolvable conflict. You seem to want a more purposeful life or sense of vocation in which your interests and God's purposes are basically compatible."

This diagnostic interpretation includes a major theme and a variation on this theme. There are, of course, a variety of ways in which a thematically informed diagnosis might be formulated and communicated in this case. One important feature of this particular formulation, however, is that it focuses both on problems relating to her belief in God and on her conflicts with other people. There is no covert assumption here that the problem of her confidence in God's providence is only apparent, that her real problem is her interpersonal relations with her family. On the contrary, this statement recognizes that these two problems are linked together. It would therefore not make any fundamental difference which of these problems were given priority in the counseling process itself. It may be as important and urgent to help her toward a deeper understanding of the grace of God as to address her in-laws' behavior toward her.

The observation that Jeanne Guyon's religious and psychological problems are dynamically related invites us to consider how Erikson's psychosocial themes might be applied to this case. Since providence, communion, and repentance are the major theological themes in this account, the primary psychosocial themes ought to be trust vs. mistrust, intimacy vs. isolation, and initiative vs. guilt. And since vocation is the theme that reflects a more positive variation on the current situation, industry vs. inferiority and generativity vs. stagnation would be the themes that merit closest observation as the counselor works toward the improvement of her current situation.

The counselor would probably find it fruitful to draw these relationships between the theological themes and the psychosocial themes. But the important point is that the theological diagnosis should be responsive to the psychological dynamics of the case. There is no need to assume that a theological and a psychological interpretation of this case would be incompatible. In fact, it can be argued that a theological diagnosis might well provide a fresher *psychological* understanding of Jeanne Guyon's current situation than many psychological interpretations would afford. As informal evidence of this, I find that when I ask students to interpret this case psychologically, many place considerable emphasis on her "martyr complex," i.e., her unaccountable need to suffer indignities without fighting back. But when I ask students to interpret the same selection theologically, they place much less emphasis on her "need to suffer" and greater emphasis on the fact that it is difficult for religious faith and commitment to flourish in such inhospitable social environments. Obviously, a theological interpretation is not to be preferred to a psychological one simply because it takes a more charitable view of the counselee. But the theological interpretations based on the seven theological themes have tended to take a more balanced view of her strengths as well as her weaknesses, and thus actually come closer to the viewpoint of the personality theories to which these students theoretically adhere.

Theology and pastoral counseling. Our emphasis on the use

of theological themes in pastoral counseling ought not be con-
strued as an attempt to develop an entirely new approach to
pastoral counseling. As early as 1961, Daniel Day Williams
analyzed one of Carl Rogers' counseling cases from a theological point of view. He concluded that the issues dealt with in
many of Rogers' counseling interviews have religious and theological implications, but

there is little explicit discussion of religious issues. The counselor
seems definitely to keep them to one side. Mrs. Oak's language at
times touches upon religious confession . . . , but for the most part,
the issues dealt with do not seem to take the form of theological
questions about the meaning of life. Attention is focused on this one
person's inner struggle, on her immediate feelings and relationships.
And the outcome seems to be stated as an inward reorganization and
recovery, not as a new structure of religious belief.[35]

Williams hastens to point out that he is not suggesting "that
the counseling of this distressed person should have proceeded
as a discussion of the theological and ethical issues" involved,
because in many cases "the immediate discussion of these
questions would only get in the way of the real discovery of the
self." But he does want to argue that "in the final analysis of
any human problem, we have to raise these ultimate religious
questions if we are to have any adequate understanding of what
fulfills a human life." Thus, Williams clearly believes that the
theological implications of counseling ought to be addressed.
Our concern here, therefore, has been to go beyond more
general discussions of the theological implications of counseling and to attempt to specify in more precise fashion the actual
theological themes to which counselees give verbal assent.
Thus, our concern here has been not only to make the general
point that theological issues are too often left unexplored in the
counseling session, but also to take a step toward identifying
the sorts of theological themes and their psychosocial correlates, that are found frequently enough in pastoral counseling
to merit more than passing interest.

The Impairment of Theological Themes

Our discussion thus far has centered on the task of identifying and communicating the theological themes that are at least implicit in the pastoral counseling session. As our illustration of Jeanne Marie Guyon shows, identification of such themes does not mean that these themes are experienced only positively by the counselee. Her experience of communion during the period of her marriage, for example, was largely negative. But it does mean that these themes, including those that are experienced negatively, have relevance to the counselee and his or her problems. There is a sense of their appropriateness, a sense that one ought to experience the providence of God, that one ought to feel repentant, etc. Thus, even if some themes are experienced in their negative form, they still help to define the context within which the counselee understands his problems and struggles to do something about them.

However, many experts in theology have been saying for some time that theological understandings no longer have the influence on the lives of individuals that they used to have. Not only do people fail to experience the positive influence of God in their lives but also they no longer experience the absence of God's positive influence as a personal lack or loss. Such persons reflect neither the positive nor the negative dimensions of the theological themes that we have been discussing here. Theological themes such as providence, faith, grace, and repentance simply lack any relevance at all.

In concluding our discussion of theological themes and pastoral counseling, I would like to explore this issue further. Thematically speaking, what these experts in theology are saying is that the traditional thematic structures on which the theological themes are based have undergone what classical Gestalt psychologists have called the "weakening of shape." It is not simply that there has been a thematic reversal—where the positive experiences of these themes have been replaced by negative experiences—but that the thematic structure as a whole has become formless.

The psychologist in the thematic tradition who has come the closest to expressing this viewpoint is Robert Jay Lifton, a psychiatrist whose writings have focused on the psychohistory of contemporary groups. While his comments on the decline of traditional theological views are only part of a larger assessment of the weakening of traditional personal and social structures, he does not exclude theological views from this general assessment. He suggests, for example, that people no longer find traditional eschatological symbols meaningful in their attempts to understand human mortality.[36] Not only do people confess to having difficulty believing these traditional views but the traditional views do not even shape their consciousness of the issue of human mortality. This example reflects Lifton's more general tendency to explore the impairment of the traditional structures of human thought and action, and to point out how new themes that evolve out of the experience of such impairment are themselves reflective of the loss of these traditional structures. New themes emerge, but they are not integrated into an identifiable thematic structure capable of replacing the old structures.

Consider, for example, Lifton's studies based on his work with the survivors of the bombing of Hiroshima.[37] The psychosocial theme that grew out of this experience was that of *survivorship* itself. Survivors were defining themselves as survivors. The others have been killed, but I have survived. In addition to the obvious fact that this experience of survival caused these individuals to raise some fundamental questions about why they had survived and what it meant to survive the destruction of one's environment, it is also evident that this theme of survival is not securely established within a thematic structure. It does not fit well with the traditional structures, especially religious and psychological, on which the culture was based. It remains an extremely powerful theme, capable of articulating how these individuals experience themselves in interaction with the environment as it now exists, but it nonetheless reflects the impairment of the thematic structures that had previously legitimated their modes of interaction with the environment. Another way to put this is that, when the environmental press is reasonably well-defined, individuals are able to respond on the basis of clearly definable needs. But Lifton is showing how survival is a theme instigated by an environmental press so fortuitous and utterly confusing that individuals were unable to react to its influence in any meaningful way. The absence of a sense of meaning or coherence in the interaction of environmental influence and personal interest is reflected in the ambiguity these victims experienced over the very theme of survivorship. Not only did the survivors have difficulty articulating what survival means but also some doubted that even this theme could be applied to them. For these, death had already occurred.

Protean man and the weakening of traditional thematic structures. Having noted how thematic structures may themselves collapse and in this collapse give rise to free-floating themes that are not securely established in either the old thematic structures or emergent new ones, I would like to consider Lifton's influential essay on "Protean man."[38] In this essay, Lifton formulates a conception of contemporary man in which the major life themes express the loss of traditional thematic structures and therefore manifest considerable ambiguity and impairment of individuals' customary interactions with their environments. In effect, Lifton argues that a new type of individual has emerged in our day, one whose interactions with his environment are characterized far more by change and disruption than by stability and constancy. Naming this new type of individual after Proteus (the figure in Greek mythology who was able to change his identity with relative ease), Lifton says that the

Protean style of self-process, then, is characterized by an interminable series of experiments and explorations—some shallow, some profound—each of which can readily be abandoned in favor of still new, psychological quests.[39]

While his clinical examples of this new type of man are largely drawn from young adults, Lifton contends that "Protean man inhabits us all. We all live in contemporary society, and are all in greater or lesser degree exposed to the forces I have mentioned." Also, while he is willing to acknowledge that men resembling Protean man have undoubtedly existed in earlier historical periods, "the extremity of recent historical developments has rendered him a much more discrete and widespread entity. That is what permits us to stress his emergence." In Lifton's judgment, the forces that have given rise to the emergence of Protean man as a collective phenomenon are *widespread historical dislocation* (or the break in the sense of connection we have felt with vital symbols of our cultural traditions) and the *flooding of imagery* (or the flow of postmodern and nontraditional cultural influences over mass communication networks). Both forces have considerably altered the customary interactions of individuals with their environments.

In reacting to these forces, individuals have taken on certain characteristics or personal themes peculiar to the Protean style. These themes do not constitute a new thematic structure of the personality; they merely reflect a varied collection of adjustments to the impairment of traditional forms of interaction with one's environment that has not resulted in a new thematic structure. Lifton identifies the following Protean themes:

1. *Individuals are starved for ideas that can give coherence to their world.* New ideas are more likely to challenge old ideas than to provide a coherent perspective on the world and one's own experience.

2. *Individuals have a strong sense of life's absurdity.* This theme focuses on individuals' mockery of themselves and of others, their perception that the activities and beliefs engaged in by one's society are strange and inappropriate.

3. *Individuals have a suspicion of false nurturance.* The breakdown of traditional institutions leads to dependence on newer institutions that the individual also mistrusts because they, too, threaten his basic autonomy.

4. *Individuals exhibit a paradoxical attitude toward technol-*

ogy. Individuals are sympathetic toward technical achievement, and employ modern technology to combat the problems posed by the preceding themes. But they are also profoundly disillusioned with science, the ultimate power behind this technology, because it is capable of massive destruction.

5. *Individuals have hidden guilt.* This theme focuses on individuals' vague but persistent sense of self-condemnation and unworthiness. This is all the more troublesome for its lack of clear origin. An individual suffers from guilt and while he lacks an awareness of the ultimate cause of his suffering, the guilt is related to his sense of having no outlet for his loyalties and no symbolic structure for his achievements.

6. *Individuals have anxiety and resentment.* This theme is related to the theme of suspicion of counterfeit nurturance (3). The individual feels betrayed, and this causes fear and anger, but he has no consistent target for his anger (e.g., a father figure). His anger is therefore diffuse and formless, now directed toward one target, now another.

7. *Change and human mortality.* This theme reflects individuals' deep ambivalence about change itself. The individual is attracted to the idea of making all things totally new— i.e., to the "mode of transformation." But he is equally drawn to an image of a mythical past of perfect harmony and pre-scientific wholeness. The ambivalence expresses itself in the impairment of the symbolism of transition within the life cycle, i.e., the *rites of passage* surrounding birth, entry into adulthood, marriage, and death. The central impairment here is that of symbolic immortality, i.e., the need for imagery of connection or continuity predating and extending beyond the individual life span.

This list of seven Protean themes and brief descriptions of each indicates that the Protean style reflects a serious impairment of the interactions that have traditionally ensued between individuals and their environments. Lifton concludes his essay on Protean man by asking whether these impairments of accustomed interactions are merely a destructive influence in the lives of modern individuals, or whether these impairments play a constructive role as well. In his view, one effect of this impairment of traditional modes of interaction between individual and environment is that Protean man values self-discovery more highly, and reflects a deeper understanding of the sheer complexity of the self process. This greater sensitivity to the complexities of the self is evidenced in his capacity to engage in self-mockery, in his refusal to oversimplify the grounds for his guilt, anxiety, and resentment, and in his search for convincing symbolic formulations of the survival of the self process over the forces of physical decay and death. On the other hand, counterbalancing this deeper understanding of the self process is the loss of coherent meaning systems, the difficulty of making commitments to existing institutions (both new and old), the mistrust of the technology and skills one employs, and the greater diffuseness in which his emotions are experienced and expressed.

Protean themes and theological themes. The overall effect of these changes, both the more positive and the more negative, is the severe impairment of the thematic structure reflected in Pruyser's theological themes. To dramatize this, the diagram on the next page shows the correspondence between Lifton's themes of Protean man and Pruyser's theological themes. Such a correlation shows that not only are one or another of these theological themes threatened by the emergence of Protean man but the total thematic structure is subjected to massive weakening of shape.

The first set of correlations concerns the presence or absence of beliefs that give life meaning and coherence. The second set of correlations concerns the problem of whether the world as one experiences it is trustworthy or absurd. The third set of correlations relates to the problem of whether one's social groups provide real support or only false nurturance. The fourth set of correlations concerns the problem of whether one's technical effectiveness is consistent with one's larger vocational intentions. The fifth set of correlations relates to the experience of guilt. The sixth set of correlations relates to an individual's sense of being upheld vs. the feeling of having been

CORRELATION OF PROTEAN AND THEOLOGICAL THEMES

Protean Themes	Theological Themes
(1) starved for ideas that provide a coherent world view	faith
(2) sense of absurdity	providence
(3) suspicion of false nurturance	communion
(4) paradoxical attitude toward technology	vocation
(5) hidden guilt	repentance
(6) anxiety and resentment	grace or gratefulness
(7) change and mortality	awareness of the holy

betrayed. The seventh set of correlations relates to man's relation to powers that transcend his own powers and control his destiny.

For our purposes here, it is not necessary to enter into the debate as to whether contemporary man is more like Lifton's Protean man or Pruyser's theological man. We need only observe that the pastoral counselor encounters individuals who either temporarily or more chronically reflect Protean themes. To the extent that this is true of a given counselee, the counselor will recognize the weakening of shape that is the consequence of the presence of these themes. And the diagnostic interpretation will appropriately center on this weakening of the thematic structure itself. As in a diagnosis that assumes the intactness of the theological thematic structure, such a diagnostic interpretation would seek to determine the Protean themes most responsible for this weakening of shape, and the theme or themes most likely to effect new variations, e.g., through the discovery of new facets of their theological correlates.

Conclusion

Our primary interest in this chapter has been to make the case that pastoral counseling is *pastoral* not merely or even primarily because it takes place in a pastoral context or setting, but because its structure of communication is theological. In Wittgenstein's term, theology is the "language game" within which the counseling takes place. By focusing on Pruyser's theological themes, we have been able to indicate that the theological content of pastoral counseling is not abstract but personal and experiential. And, by considering Lifton's Protean themes in terms of the notion of the "weakening of shape," we have been able to show that even in the case of counselees whose lives are not lived out of the assumptions on which the theological themes are based, the counseling session retains its theological structure. Theological themes in this case are the thematic variations that function like rumors of angels: possibilities that are only a step removed from verbal articulation.[40]

5
Thematic Dimensions
of Personal and Group Crises

In her book *Poetic Closure*, Barbara Herrnstein Smith identifies three major types of thematic structure in poetry. The first involves *repetition* of themes, the second is *sequential*, and the third is *dialectical*. [41] The familiar song "Billy Boy" is an example of a thematic structure based on repetition: "Can she fry a dish of meat?" "Can she make a loaf of bread?" "Can she feed a sucking pig?" and so on. A more complex thematic pattern is the sequential form. There are poems, for example, whose thematic structure involves temporal sequence (birth—infancy—youth—manhood—old age—death) and others whose thematic structure involves logical sequence ("if . . . then"; "either . . . or"). A third form of thematic structure is *dialectical*. This form is reflected in poems that capture the hesitant shiftings and gropings of a mind struggling with a complex intellectual or moral issue and attempting to think it through to a stable conclusion. Hamlet's soliloquy, "To be or not to be, that is the question . . ." is reflective of the dialectical structure.

Throughout this study, we have been focusing primarily on the first (and simplest) form of thematic pattern, i.e., repetition. We have noted how both individuals and groups function in terms of repeated or recurrent themes, and we have noted that change in the thematic patterns of individuals and groups involves variations on these recurrent themes. In this concluding chapter, I would like to give more attention to the other two forms of thematic structure, the sequential and the dialectical, and to explore their implications for pastoral care in crisis situations.

As indicated earlier, Erikson's life cycle theory incorporates both sequential and dialectical thematic structures. While the psychosocial themes in his life cycle theory do not manifest an *invariant* sequence, they are nonetheless sequential in a certain sense. A theme is not limited to a specific stage in life, yet the themes are intended to chart personal development from birth to infancy to childhood to adolescence to young adulthood to adulthood to old age. Thus, the thematic structure of Erikson's life cycle includes temporal sequence. While it is sometimes argued that Erikson's life cycle theory fails to take adequate account of the crises in late childhood and middle adulthood, it nonetheless covers all the stages in life from birth to old age and does so in temporal sequence. The very possibility of an individual varying the sequence (through recapitulation or anticipation) depends on the existence of the sequence itself.

We have also noted that Erikson's life cycle theory has a dialectical feature. This is evident in his formulation of the psychosocial themes in terms of contrasting dimensions: trust vs. mistrust, autonomy vs. shame and self-doubt, and so on. This incorporates into the life cycle theory an appreciation of the hesitant shiftings and gropings of the individual struggling with complex life tasks and attempting to work them through to a stable resolution.

By noting that Erikson's life cycle theory has sequential and dialectical features, we have a basis for exploring some of the more complex dimensions of the thematic structures encountered in pastoral work. If we work only with the repetition model of thematic structures, we neglect the role that sequence and dialectic play in the shaping of the thematic structures of individuals and groups. What is happening in an individual or group, for example, when normal expectations of temporal sequence are disrupted—whether because the sequence is terminated before it has an opportunity to go full term, or because elements in the sequence have gotten out of order? Or what is happening in an individual or group when its usual tendency to operate in terms of repetition (i.e., performing as it has performed in the past) is threatened, causing it to move into a dialectical pattern involving the search for a new basis on which to constitute itself?

The practice of pastoral care requires considerable attention to these disruptions. The "crisis" dimension of pastoral care is precisely related to these disruptions or aberrations in thematic structures. If, for example, an individual is normally expected to complete the whole temporal sequence of life from birth to old age, death at one of the earlier stages poses a crisis situation inasmuch as the temporal sequence has not been completed. Many of the issues that vex the theory and practice of pastoral care relate to this problem of the disruption or untimely termination of the normal temporal sequence: abortion, accidental death, suicide, and euthanasia.

The crisis dimension of pastoral care also relates to the dialectical pattern. Divorce, for example, involves the breakdown of a marital pattern that manifested thematic repetition. Now, the divorced person is cast into a dialectical pattern that involves groping for new forms of clarity and insight. Occupational or professional retirement is another example of this change from a pattern of repetition to a pattern based on dialectic.

By identifying types of thematic structures, we are able to make a place for such crises in a thematic understanding of pastoral care. The more difficult task, however, is to determine how the thematic approach can help the minister use such crises to effect personal change. I will therefore discuss two cases, one in which the normal temporal sequence of life threatens to be disrupted, and another in which the customary thematic pattern of repetition gives way to a dialectical structure. The first case centers on the life of an individual, the second on a local congregation.

The Disruption of Temporal Sequence: Sara Graham

The first case is taken from Evans and Parker's *Christian Theology.*[42] It is an account of a sixteen-year-old girl named Sara Graham who is suffering from a kidney disease. The question she begins to struggle with after two unsuccessful kidney transplants is whether to continue to make the effort to live through the use of a dialysis machine or simply to let matters take their natural course. Without the artificial cleansing of her blood through dialysis she could live only a few weeks. If she continued the treatment, there was a chance she could live for at least a few more years. The case is related from the perspective of Sara's older sister, Tracy Graham.

Unsuccessful Medical Treatment. Tracy, now seventeen, and Sara, who would be sixteen next month, had always been very close. It.was now almost six months to the day when Sara had begun to lose weight and get very weak. The family doctor said it was a kidney disease and had recommended Dr. Adams, a specialist. When both of Sara's kidneys failed, she was put on a dialysis machine which hooks up to the blood circulation system and cleans the blood of impurities as the kidneys would. Dr. Adams began to look for a donor to give Sara a healthy kidney.

Tracy remembered the arguments with her parents. She wanted to be the donor, but her mom, dad, and Sara, as well as Dr. Adams, said "no." A donor was at last found, the transplant made, but after ten days of waiting the signs were obvious that Sara's body would reject the new kidney. She was placed back on the dialysis machine. Tracy insisted again that she be the next donor. As there was a slightly better chance of her kidney being accepted, the girls' parents and Sara reluctantly agreed. Three weeks later Tracy's transplanted kidney was also rejected by Sara's body. . . .

Dr. Adams had called Mr. and Mrs. Graham and Tracy into Sara's room for a conference. He told the family then that some blunt realities had to be faced. "After two rejections, we should no longer consider a kidney transplant as a possibility at this time. In a few days when Sara is stronger, she will be able to go home and resume many of her normal activities. But she must return here to the hospital three days a week for six to eight hours to use the dialysis machine. If not, her own blood would poison her. At the present time there is no medication that can take the place of this machine. However, there is always the hope that through new medical advances we will learn how to combat the rejection of an organ transplant." Dr. Adams had told the family in confidence yesterday that Sara might live only a short time even with dialysis because of the possibility of several complications that could arise.

Plans for the future. The Grahams began to make plans for the future. At this point the purchase of a dialysis machine was financially an impossibility for them, and in their part of the state none was available for rental. Thus because the family lived more than sixty-five miles from the hospital, Mr. Graham, who ran a small business in Oak Town, began to look for an apartment much closer to the city. Tracy knew that the medical costs for Sara had placed the family heavily in debt. The members of their village church, many of whom had been regular visitors at the hospital for the past few months, had spoken of their prayers for her, and had already held two bazaars to raise money for Sara's expenses. The money had covered only a fraction of the actual costs. Mrs. Graham, who spent her days with Sara in the hospital, had begun to take in secretarial work in the evenings. Tracy, now in her senior year of high school, said that she really didn't want to go off to school in the fall, but would rather postpone this and get a job instead.

Sara told Tracy how aware she was of the love and support of the family and their friends. She said she was most aware of the tremendous faith they had in things working out for the best. Recently Sara had spoken to Tracy several times of their common Christian beliefs and of her assurance of a life after death. Dr. Adams had told her how lucky she was to have access to the machine. But Sara confessed to Tracy that the idea of living through the machine was very hard to take. . . .

Sara was quite thin and took many days to recover from her second surgery. She had gotten acquainted with Mike, a boy on the same floor, and had told Tracy about him. "He's just a little guy. He's really twelve, but he looks about nine. He's waiting for a kidney donor, but unless one shows up pretty soon, he'll need the machine to make it. I even explained to him what the machine does. But I overheard two of the nurses talking. Right now there's no space available to schedule Mike for dialysis. Do you know that only one out of ten people who need this machine gets a chance, and our hospital has one of the only machines like this in our section of the state?"

That was over a week ago. Then just this morning, Sara had turned to Tracy and in a clear, firm voice said, "Trace, I can't stand the thought of living the rest of my life tied to this machine. It's not living for me. I want to go home now—and not come back to the hospital. I've already told Mom and Dad. They are very sad, but I think they understand. But most important to me is that *you* understand and will support my decision."

Temporal sequence and psychosocial themes. In discussing this case, our concern is to determine how the thematic approach to personality can assist the pastor in working toward personal change in crisis situations. In initiating this discussion, we will take some of our cues from the theologians who wrote about this case.[43] All three theologians agree that the case is about hope. The first theologian puts it this way:

What did Sara find in her Christian faith that made her free to die? How could she look forward to the future with the assurance of eternal life rather than the fear of death? Those around her—family, friends, and medical specialists—looked on Sara's predicament as a problem to be solved. They were willing to make extreme sacrifices to do their part. Not unappreciative of these efforts, Sara was able to transcend the level of ambiguity at which they coped with her "case."[44]

The second theologian, who also agrees that the case is about hope, nonetheless disagrees with the first theologian's view that Sara found in her Christian faith a transcendent hope. He argues that "The Christian hope breaks through Sara's anxiety only intermittently and uncertainly. . . . Sara had, to be sure, spoken to Tracy of 'their common Christian beliefs and of her assurance of a life after death,' but without further elucidation this sentiment seems a slim line on which to suspend confident hope in the invisible world." This theologian goes on to argue that Sara seemed to have some confidence in "God's general providence and purpose," but "how much more it would mean to know herself bracketed by God's love in the midst of misfortune and at the borders of death." The third theologian also agrees that, theologically speaking, the case is about hope. But she is critical of the individualistic understanding of hope presented in this case. She points out that the Biblical framework of hope "does not start with the individual, but with the community and with the created world." Thus, this case presents an individual drama of death:

The individual appears as an isolated "case" to make her decision, without a context in a community of faith, a cosmic project of life. To confine one's comment on biblical eschatology to the terms presented to us by this story is virtually to predetermine a theology of personal immortality rather than a theology of biblical hope.[45]

If we place these theological judgments within the context of Erikson's psychosocial themes, we may say that this case is about trust vs. mistrust, with its corresponding virtue of hope (and its related theological theme of providence). Erikson's theme of intimacy vs. isolation, with its corresponding virtue of love, is also relevant, because two of the three theologians felt Sara's understanding of hope was not adequately integrated into a larger sense of human and divine communion. Thus, by looking at Sara's illness in terms of the temporal sequence of human life as described in Erikson's life cycle theory, we gain the following insights into her situation: The normal temporal sequence of life would place this sixteen-year-old girl in the identity vs. identity diffusion stage, with its corresponding virtue of fidelity (and its parallel theological theme of faith). In her illness, however, she reclaims the tacit knowledge she acquired in the first stage of her life when she first experienced themes of trust, hope, and providence. Her decision to relinquish her life is based on the fiduciary hold that these themes exert on her life and her religious faith. On the other hand, the theologians are saying in effect that her failure to locate this knowledge within the larger context of human and divine communion reflects an inability to anticipate themes ordinarily encountered at a later stage of the temporal sequence. In their view, she has not projected her thoughts and convictions forward to the intimacy vs. isolation stage, with its corresponding virtue of love (and parallel theological theme of communion). Thus, while her recovery of trust, hope, and providence has been critical to her continuing religious faith in extremely difficult times, the theological critiques of this case are saying that she also needs to work through the implications of the intimacy vs. isolation stage.

By placing these theological critiques in the context of Erikson's psychosocial themes, we can begin to understand what happens to individuals in crises that involve the disruption of the temporal sequence of their lives. In thematic terms, these crises force individuals to give particular emphasis to themes normally emphasized at an earlier or later stage in the temporal sequence. In Sara's case, this meant reclaiming the trust, hope, and sense of God's providence that were vouchsafed to her in infancy. But such reclamation is only part of the task that confronts her. The other and more difficult task is to project her life forward and to experience those stages of life that are not yet a part of her experience. Thus, not only do crises of this nature disrupt the normal sequence of life, but they require the individual to address life's themes without regard to their normal or appropriate sequence.

However, unlike the two theologians who are critical of Sara's inadequate grasp of the communal dimension of her hope, I would argue that she has already begun to address those life themes (both in their psychosocial and theological dimensions) which she has not directly experienced. For example, she tells her sister Tracy how aware she is "of the love and support of the family and their friends." This concern indicates that she has in fact anticipated the theme of *intimacy vs. isolation*, with its corrollary themes of love and communion. Furthermore, in reflecting on her responsibilities to her family and friends, especially in the light of their own sacrifices in her behalf, she has struggled with the fundamental dynamic of the intimacy vs. isolation stage, i.e., the individual's capacity to make commitments to concrete affiliations that call for significant sacrifices and compromises. In a similar way, she has also confronted the subsequent theme of *generativity vs. stagnation*.

Generativity is reflected in her concern for the life of young Mike, who may be needing the dialysis machine, and concern for stagnation is reflected in the thought "of living the rest of my life tied to this machine. Its not living for me." She has even struggled with the final theme of *integrity vs. despair.* As one of the theologians puts it, "When death itself becomes a reflective act, an act of conscious self-completion, our fears and the tears of those around us are stilled by our encounter with a deeper unity." In this act of reflection, Sara has had to consider the question of her own integrity. As Erikson describes the integrity that one normally experiences in the final stage of life:

It is the acceptance of one's own and only life cycle and of the people who have become significant to it as something that had to be and that, by necessity, permitted of no substitutions. It thus means a different love of one's parents, free of the wish that they should have been different, and an acceptance of the fact that one's life is one's own responsibility.[46]

In accepting her fate and assuming responsibility for her life, Sara reflects the personal integrity characteristic of the final stage of life. It may be that she also reflects despair, "the feeling that the time is short, too short for the attempt to start another life," i.e., the life of the semi-invalid "tied to this machine." The important point, however, is that she has been struggling with the themes of adulthood. She has not had the luxury of confronting these themes in their normal sequence. If the pastor is sensitive to the added thematic complexity that occurs when a crisis disrupts the normal temporal sequence of life, he will be in a better position to help an individual integrate both past and future themes into a unique personal style, rather than allowing the crisis to hasten the disintegration of these themes into mere contradiction.

In short, one major type of crisis having implications for pastoral care involves disruption of temporal sequence. The effect of such disruption is that life themes, normally experienced in regular sequence, are confronted in a very differ-

ent manner. Themes experienced earlier are attended to with
renewed passion, and themes typically met with in later stages
of life are no longer deferrable. Because crises evoke a variety
of themes, they are thematically complex. They are rich with
possibilities for personal change that far exceed those of variations on a single theme. They are also unusually threatening
because the negative dimensions of themes are necessarily
compounded. A crisis such as the one confronting Sara and the
Graham family disrupts the normal temporal sequence of life
and, in so doing, disrupts the normal relationship between
themes and life experience. The pastor's task here is complicated by the fact that themes are confronted without the
support of the life experiences that normally sustain them.

Thematic Structure as Dialectical Pattern: Ann Hibbens

The disruption of temporal sequence is one of two types of
crisis under consideration here. The other type involves the
thematic structure that is dialectical in nature. The dialectical
structure is the most complex thematic structure among the
three major types, i.e., repetition, sequential, and dialectical.
The dialectical structure may appear to lack the thematic coherence of the other two types, but this is only apparent. The
dialectical structure has thematic coherence, but it is based on
an internal tension or conflict attributable to the complexity of
the ideas, feelings, or intentions it addresses.

An instance of the dialectical pattern that bears directly on
the issue of crisis occurs when the customary pattern of thematic repetition breaks down and the individual or group is cast
into a dialectical situation involving much hesitancy and groping. Routine repetition of patterns gives way to tension.
Clearly, not all instances of the dialectical pattern are the result
of the breakdown of the pattern of repetition, but this is a
relatively familiar phenomenon in both individual and group
processes, and thus is not unusual in the life of the local congregation.

The excommunication of Ann Hibbens. I would like to explore an example of this phenomenon in the life of a local congregation, again employing Erikson's psychosocial themes to clarify it. This example is based on an episode in the life of First Church of Boston in 1640.[47] The event was the excommunication proceedings against one of its members, Ann Hibbens. Mrs. Hibbens, the wife of a wealthy and politically influential merchant, was one of the first residents of Boston. In September 1640, excommunication proceedings were instituted against her by First Church over an incident involving a bitter quarrel with a carpenter whom she had hired to do work in her house. The carpenter had agreed to do the work for a certain price, but Mrs. Hibbens asked him to do some additional work for which she agreed to pay extra. When she received the total bill, she complained that it was excessive. Another carpenter, a member of First Church, was called in to arbitrate and arrived at a negotiated figure that satisfied the original carpenter and Mr. Hibbens but not Mrs. Hibbens. She contended that the two carpenters acted in collusion, that the negotiator arrived at a figure on which the two of them had agreed in advance. The negotiator vigorously denied this charge and, when the dispute became unresolvable, Mrs. Hibbens was brought before the whole church body to respond to charges brought against her by the carpenter who had served as the arbitrator. During the hearings in September 1640, she was admonished by the church to mend her contentious ways or face further, more severe action. Five months later, in February 1641, the church membership concluded that she remained unrepentant and arrived at the decision to excommunicate her. After her excommunication, she does not appear in the historical record for more than a decade. However, her husband died in 1654 and with his death she lost his personal influence in the community, which had shielded her from the full weight of her neighbors' hatred. Two years after his death, she was convicted in the general courts on a charge of witchcraft and was sentenced to death. The evidence presented in support of the witchcraft charge was the claim that she had an uncanny ability to hear what her neighbors were saying when they were out of normal hearing range.

As we explore this case as a dialectical process, I want to draw attention to Erikson's comment regarding the relationship between the autonomy vs. shame and self-doubt stage and the initiative vs. guilt stage. In *Childhood and Society* he comments, "Shame is an emotion insufficiently studied, because in our civilization it is so early and easily absorbed by guilt."[48] In the life of First Church of Boston, the dominant theme is that of initiative vs. guilt. The church's theology and polity are largely centered around issues of sin, retribution, forgiveness, etc. However, in the episode involving Ann Hibbens, this normal pattern of interaction was severely disrupted and the church was thrown into a more dialectical situation in which the theme of autonomy vs. shame and self-doubt assumed special importance and came to have a controlling influence on the church's proceedings. The conflict this created within the congregation itself was resolved in the negative side of the autonomy vs. shame and self-doubt conflict. Mrs. Hibbens was consigned to public humiliation through censure and excommunication. Thus, while the church normally handled its affairs in terms of initiative vs. guilt, the Hibbens affair cast it into a major dialectical crisis in which autonomy vs. shame and self-doubt replaces initiative vs. guilt as the controlling theme.

The verbatim account of Mrs. Hibbens' excommunication was written by the congregation's secretary. In the following thematic analysis, quotations are from this official record of the proceedings. The proceedings had been initiated in order to determine whether Mrs. Hibbens was guilty in the dispute over the carpentry work. As the church secretary put it, "Mrs. Hibbens was to be called into question for some offense which she had given to some brethren and [about which she] would not be convinced. It was now to be told to the church [in order] that it may judge of it." After the charges against her were lodged, Mrs. Hibbens was asked by the pastor to respond to them. When she failed to do so (apparently because she had turned "aside to talk with this Brother or that Brother"), the discussion shifted from the original charges against her to this second act of impertinence. When one of her supporters said that Mrs. Hibbens did not speak because it is unlawful for women to speak in the church, the pastor replied that "it is lawful for a woman to speak when she is asked a question." When the proceedings were resumed the following Sunday, Mrs. Hibbens confessed to impropriety in her failure to respond to the charges lodged against her the previous week, but she contended that she was not guilty of the original charges and asked to be allowed to respond to the charges in writing. Her request was rejected on the grounds that it lacked Scriptural precedent, and the pastor strongly admonished her to proceed immediately with her defense:

Therefore, Sister, you shall do well to express yourself, for the thing laid to your charge is [a] matter of crime and sin; and that may either be acknowledged or cleared, and by writing things would be drawn on to a further length, when the Brethren hath been too long already delayed in the answer and the church hath many other business— [such] as to proceed with our Brethren at the island, which we would willingly do the next Lord's Day.[49]

She proceeded with her defense, but it was not well received. As the pastor put it, "All this you now relate is only to excuse yourself, and lessen your own fault, and lay blame upon others." When she protested that a carpenter from Salem had judged that she had been grossly overcharged for the carpentry work, various elders complained that they had heard enough from her. One said that everything she had spoken "tends not to any measure of repentance or sorrow for her sin." Another said that her worst crime was to take the issue in her own hands and not allow her husband to handle the dispute with the carpenter, "as if she were able to manage it better than her husband, which is a plain breach of the rule of Christ." After a number of similar speeches, the pastor proceeded with his charge against her. The decision was made to censure her rather than formally excommunicate her from the church. However, five months later she was again brought before the church because she had been saying in the community that the church had dealt unfairly with her in the earlier proceedings. Because she was still unrepentant, the pastor and elders decided that no useful purpose would be served by allowing her more time to repent inasmuch as "all her speeches hath tended to excuse herself and to lay all blame upon others—as upon our honored magistrate Mr. Winthrop, upon our Elders and the revered elders of other churches. . . ." The pastor therefore proceeded with the excommunication.

From repetition to dialectical pattern. Throughout these proceedings, the issues of sin, guilt, repentance, and retribution were prominent at the formal level of deliberation. However, as Mrs. Hibbens refused to accept responsibility for the conflict and would not acknowledge her sin, a subterranean theme more related to issues of shame began to enter into the proceedings. For example, in the earlier proceedings which led to her censure, two or three parishioners expressed the desire "to help on the work of humiliation upon her heart," and one added that he did so because she sought to "hide" her sin. Later the same day the pastor, in his charge of censure, criticized her for having "uttered words tending to the disgrace and defamation of your Brethren." Then, during the proceedings that led to her excommunication, one parishioner compared Mrs. Hibbens to Moses' sister Miriam,

who rose up against Moses and Aaron [and] whose leprosy appeared in the face of the congregation. And there was a law for lepers that the priest should search and view them; and if upon the search they found leprosy appearing, the priest was to pronounce them lepers, and then they were to be thrust out for a time till they were healed of that disease for the [sake of the] congregation and the society of God's people. As this Sister hath been diligently searched and viewed and upon the search she is found leprous and diverse spots are risen and do manifestly appear to the congregation, therefore, according to the law of God, I think she ought to be pronounced unclean and as a leprous person to be put out from amongst us.[50]

The pastor appeared to agree with this assessment of Mrs. Hibbens as a shameful person, because in his excommunication pronouncement he concluded:

I do here . . . pronounce you to be a leprous and unclean person. . . . You have scorned counsel and refused instruction and have like a filthy swine trampled those pearls under your feet. . . . And so as an unclean beast and unfit for the society of God's people, I do from this time forward pronounce you an excommunicated person from God and His people.[51]

These statements by parishioners and pastor introduce the dynamics of shame into a decision-making process that is formally focused on issues of guilt. And while these excerpts cannot convey the full force of it, there is an emotional intensity to these statements about shame that is largely missing from the statements relating to guilt. Thus, the routine use of guilt in the church's formulation of its theology and polity has been threatened by Mrs. Hibbens' refusal to accept the view that she is guilty. In the impasse that follows, guilt remains a formal issue in the deliberations, but the process is now cast into a more dialectical structure in which shaming is introduced as a complicating dynamic in the overall process. The routine thematic pattern of guilt that is normally effective in securing parishioners' cooperation and support was now being threatened. When confronted with this threat, the congregational leaders resorted to shaming devices to secure the compliance they were unable to achieve through guilt mechanisms.

On the basis of studies of New England Puritanism by historian John Demos, we should not be surprised that this occurred.[52] Demos has argued that the autonomy vs. shame and self-doubt conflict was a persistent theme in New England society in the seventeenth century. In his view, child-rearing practices among Puritans had the effect of creating severe conflicts of autonomy vs. shame and self-doubt. The key element in Puritan child-rearing patterns is the fact that for a period of perhaps twelve months the infant was treated indulgently and then, in the second year of life, was subjected to weaning, the arrival of a younger sibling and, most important of all, to a radical shift toward a harsh and restrictive style of discipline having one primary objective, i.e., to curb and even break the child's inherent "willfulness" as soon as it first began to appear. Shaming was characteristically employed as a disciplinary method in this regard, and Demos stresses the role of humiliation in Puritan child-rearing procedures, noting that "in Erikson's terms, the determination to crush the child's will is nothing less than an effort to deprive him of a chance to develop a lasting and confident sense of autonomy."

The pastor's role. Given our concern here with pastoral care in crisis situations, it is noteworthy that the reasons Pastor Cotton found the Hibbens case threatening are typical of pastor-parishioner relations today. First, Mrs. Hibbens' failure to respond when he called on her the first day was clearly a challenge to his own *authority.* When another parishioner offered as her reason for silence St. Paul's strictures against women speaking in the church, the pastor promptly informed this parishioner that, St. Paul notwithstanding, when the pastor calls upon an individual to speak, he expects that person to answer. Second, the Hibbens affair also challenged the *church's operating procedures.* When Mrs. Hibbens proposed the alternative of writing her response to the charges against her, Pastor Cotton was quick to defend the existing procedures on Scriptural grounds without exploring the possible merits of her proposal. Third, there was the fact that this case threatened Cotton's desire to maintain *the harmonious functioning of the institution itself.* One reason for not allowing her to bring in a written statement the next week was that the church had "other business" to attend to. He noted that the Hibbens case was already taking more time than he had originally planned and that it threatened other planned activities (e.g., the trip to the island). Fourth, the Hibbens affair threatened the *church's relations in the community.* One charge leveled against Mrs. Hibbens was that she sowed discord and jealousy "not only between Brethren but between our church and others, our Elders and others." In short, Pastor Cotton was personally and

professionally threatened by the Hibbens case, and this contributed to his own acceptance of the role of the adult who
breaks the "willfulness" of the errant child by shaming her into
submission.

*Meeting dialectical crises through metaphorical thought and
action.* The question this case poses, especially in the light of
the fact that these proccedings paved the way for Mrs. Hibbens' death fifteen years later, is: How might it have been
handled differently? Could something have been done during
the proceedings to alter the eventual outcome? That the process became more dialectical is not itself to be viewed negatively. The fluidity, groping, and uncertainty that are characteristic of the dialectical pattern could have issued in a creative
handling of this case. Some insights into how this might have
occurred are provided by the dialectical process in poetry. For
in poetry, the uncertainty, hesitancy, and groping that occur
in the dialectical pattern are typically worked through by
means of a poetic *metaphor*. The metaphor does not settle the
intellectual, moral, or emotional dilemma the poet is struggling
with, but it reflects his achievement of clarity as regards the
problem, providing him a satisfying sense of having confronted
the problem with some measure of perspicacity and insight.

John Keats's struggle to come to terms with his own impending death through his poetry is illustrative of the
power of the metaphor to enable an individual to confront
a difficult, even insoluble, problem and to gain some degree
of mastery over it. One dilemma that Keats struggled with
as he anticipated his own death concerned the fact that
man is capable only of brief and intermittent moments of
self-transcending awareness.[53] Man looks into the heavens
to discern a lost but benevolent presence, but this discovery
is always short-lived. The "presence" does not survive the
moment of contemplation. But Keats worked through this
dilemma, and thereby gained some mastery over his own
impending death, by means of a metaphor. In his sonnet
"Bright Star! Would I Were Steadfast as Thou Art" he
fashioned a metaphor that reversed his earlier observance of

the stars by envisioning the stars themselves as the timeless observers. As Aileen Ward points out:

> The star looking down on the sea through all time thus becomes his supreme metaphor, the formula of a state of awareness toward which his own life moved by successive stages of "annulling self".
> . . . The stars are no longer watched but become the watchers. The mortal who tries to read the "huge cloudy symbols" upon "the night's starr'd face" sees no such wonders as the stars themselves have seen in gazing eternally upon the earth, as Keats describes them—remote yet absorbed, patient or smiling, throbbing with joy or holding their breath in excitement.[54]

In this supreme metaphor, Keats is able to bring the dialectical process to a point of genuine clarity and insight. The stars are the eternal observers, and knowing this, man achieves a degree of self-transcending awareness that he fails to acquire by focusing on his own efforts at observation or contemplation.

A similar outcome might have occurred in the Hibbens case if there had been a similar metaphorical development. Admittedly, some metaphorical reflection occurred in the original case, and this reflection contributed to its outcome. Metaphors that portray Mrs. Hibbens as a leper like Miriam and as a swine before whom the church's pearls have been cast, indicate that the congregation wants to use metaphors to gain mastery over the ambiguity this case has aroused. But these metaphors grossly oversimplify the complexity of the situation. Not only is Mrs. Hibbens' role far more complex than these metaphors of leper and filthy swine indicate but also these metaphors are not accurate reflections of the issue that has come before the congregation. In an attempt to propose a metaphor closer to the circumstances of the case, Pastor Cotton in his sermon on the first day of the proceedings centered on the seventh chapter of Luke. This sermon presumably included references to verses 36–50, the story of the sinful woman who anointed Jesus' feet with oil. However, when applied to the Hibbens case, this metaphor already assumes that Mrs. Hibbens is guilty, and prescribes the appropriate response, thus communicating to the congregation that the case is a simple, unambiguous one of guilt and the need for an act of repentance.

A metaphor that would be more reflective of the issue before the congregation is Jesus' parable of the unscrupulous judge and the importunate widow. In this parable, the judge continues to refuse the widow's request for money owed to her and then finally relents, saying, "Maybe I have neither fear of God nor respect for man, but since she keeps pestering me I must give this widow her just rights, or she will persist in coming and worry me to death" (Luke 18:5, *Jerusalem Bible*). The pastor might make reference to this parable during the proceedings or he might simply let it guide his own actions. Either way, it has application to Mrs. Hibbens' behavior not only toward the carpenters but also in the excommunication proceedings. He might observe that like the widow in the parable, she would not let him off the hook. If only she could have been penitent so that they could close the case and go home. He might also choose to mention, however, that he often feels placed in the position of a judge whose supplicants would, if he permitted it, persist in worrying him to death. He might contrast his situation to that of Christ (who at least died for a purpose) and conclude that he does not want to treat the conflict between Mrs. Hibbens and the carpenters lightly, but he wonders why the pastor is always placed in the position of being a judge for people who are fully capable of solving problems of this nature by themselves. Thus he may refuse to censure or excommunicate Mrs. Hibbens not because she has established her innocence but because he is determined to be her pastor, not her parent or judge.

From this refusal to be her judge, he might propose a number of alternative courses of action. Perhaps he and Mrs. Hibbens could discuss the problem privately (a pastoral counseling approach). He might arrange for a conference between the carpenters, Mr. and Mrs. Hibbens, and himself (an administrative approach). He and Mrs. Hibbens might discuss the matter of the local carpenters' price structures with a representative group of craftsmen and businessmen in the community (a social action approach). Or he might propose forming a group

for husbands whose wives—as one male parishioner put it—
believe they are "able to manage better" than their husbands
(an institutional approach). But whatever the approach chosen,
the pastor's refusal to be "worried to death" by contentiousness
of this sort makes these approaches possible.

This resolution of the issue may beg many of the important
theological and ecclesiastical issues involved in this case.
Nonetheless, it illustrates how the extended metaphor of Jesus'
parable of the unscrupulous judge and the importunate widow
brings clarity to an ambiguous, dialectical situation. It does this
not by *applying* the parable to the situation (as the story of
Miriam the leper was merely *applied*), but by identifying a
central theme in the parable that has direct and unambiguous
relevance to the case at hand, i.e., the theme of the persistent
woman. Then, like the judge in the parable, the pastor recognizes that there needs to be a variation on this theme as it has
been enacted to date. If the theme continues in its customary
fashion, the minister and the congregation will be worried to
death by this issue. But if the pastor refuses to engage in the
process of breaking the "will" of this persistent woman, a more
constructive variation on the theme can result.

The actual solution to the problem need not exactly correspond to that of the judge in Jesus' parable. The pastor does
not, for example, order the carpenter to reduce his bill or return
Mrs. Hibbens' money. In fact, the point of viewing the parable
as an extended metaphor is precisely not to suggest that the
solution fixed upon by the judge needs to be made a general
congregational policy. Rather, the object of this use of metaphorical reflection is to enable the congregation to make their
way through to a new level of clarity concerning the dialectical
situation they confront, and then to act responsibly on the basis
of these new insights.

Conclusion

In Chapter 4, we saw how theological themes may be useful
in *diagnosing* pastoral situations. Metaphorical reflection also

has a diagnostic function as it clarifies situations of dialectical complexity. There is need for further investigation into the potential uses of metaphorical reflection in pastoral care. This type of reflection bridges some of the gaps that continue to exist between psychosocial and theological modes of pastoral diagnosis. However, our immediate concern here has been to suggest ways in which the thematic approach can enable the pastor to deal more effectively with crises in individual and corporate life. We have tried to suggest that the thematic approach to pastoral care is applicable to crisis situations.

Crises may seriously threaten the personality structures of individuals and local churches. But through awareness of the major types of thematic patterns—repetition, sequence, and dialectic—the pastor can have a better sense of how crises may contribute to personal and corporate growth. It is true that crises precipitate more complex patterns of psychosocial interaction in personal and church life. But this increased complexity need not mean that the personality structure will disintegrate into mere contradiction or massive weakening of shape. It can also mean the formation of new integrations that are more reflective of the individual's or the church's unique and enduring interests.

Psychosocial themes provide the pastor a means of discerning where there is potential for personal or corporate growth through the changes in psychosocial interaction precipitated by crises. Moreover, if a person's awareness of the life stages and their psychosocial themes can help to reduce his anxiety about crises he will confront in his own personal development, a similar awareness of the value of psychosocial themes in clarifying crisis situations in ministry will enable the pastor to anticipate future crises with more confidence and less foreboding. In turn, this confidence should allow the pastor to work with greater assurance and freedom in the present.

Notes

1. Henry A. Murray *et al., Explorations in Personality* (Oxford University Press, 1938); Henry A. Murray, ed., *Myth and Mythmaking* (George Braziller, Inc., 1960).
2. Robert W. White, *Lives in Progress,* 3d ed. (Holt, Rinehart & Winston, Inc., 1975), pp. 150–151.
3. Erik H. Erikson, *Identity and the Life Cycle* (International Universities Press, Inc., 1959), pp. 50–100; Erik H. Erikson, *Childhood and Society,* 2d ed., revised (W. W. Norton & Company, Inc., 1963), pp. 247–274.
4. Erikson, *Identity and the Life Cycle,* p. 52.
5. Paul W. Pruyser, *The Minister as Diagnostician* (The Westminster Press, 1976), p. 96.
6. For autobiographical selections that illustrate these four themes, see Donald Capps and Walter H. Capps, eds., *The Religious Personality* (Wadsworth Publishing Company, Inc., 1970).
7. Nehemiah Curnock, ed., *The Journal of the Rev. John Wesley, A.M., Vol. I* (London: The Epworth Press, 1909), pp. 313–337.
8. See Robert L. Moore, "Justification Without Joy: Psychohistorical Reflections on John Wesley's Childhood and Conversion," *History of Childhood Quarterly,* Vol. 2, pp. 31–52.
9. Erik H. Erikson, *Young Man Luther* (W. W. Norton & Company, Inc., 1958); Erik H. Erikson, *Gandhi's Truth* (W. W. Norton & Company, Inc., 1969).
10. Erikson, *Childhood and Society,* pp. 112–186.
11. *Ibid.,* pp. 147–149.
12. Richard L. Bushman, "Jonathan Edwards as Great Man: Identity, Conversion, and Leadership in the Great Awakening," *Soundings,* Vol. 52, pp. 383–396.
13. Robert A. Evans and Thomas D. Parker, eds., *Christian Theology: A Case Method Approach* (Harper and Row, Publishers, 1976), pp. 192–211.

This case was written by Robert A. Evans and Alice Frazer Evans. (Headings have been supplied.) Used by permission of Robert A. Evans and Alice Frazer Evans.

14. The theologians, in the order cited, are Robert A. Evans, Richard P. McBrien, and Owen C. Thomas.

15. Evans and Parker, eds., *Christian Theology*, p. 198.

16. "Growth and the Crises of the Healthy Personality," Erik H. Erikson, *Identity and the Life Cycle*, pp. 74–82; "Human Strength and the Cycle of Generations," Erik H. Erikson, *Insight and Responsibility* (W. W. Norton & Company, Inc., 1964), pp. 111–132.

17. James E. Dittes, *The Church in the Way* (Charles Scribner's Sons, 1967).

18. Erikson, *Childhood and Society*, pp. 223–224.

19. There are significant parallels between the approach developed here and Peter Loewenberg's use of the notion of "cohort" themes in "The Psychohistorical Origins of the Nazi Youth Cohort," *The American Historical Review*, Vol. 76, pp. 1457–1502.

20. Louis L. Martz, *The Poetry of Meditation*, rev. ed. (Yale University Press, 1962), pp. 25–39.

21. Louis L. Martz, *The Poem of the Mind* (Oxford University Press, 1966), pp. 37–38.

22. Martz, *The Poetry of Meditation*, p. 39.

23. Owen C. Watkins, *The Puritan Experience: Studies in Spiritual Autobiography* (Schocken Books, Inc., 1972), pp. 43–46.

24. *Ibid.*, p. 45.

25. Carl R. Rogers, *Client-Centered Therapy* (Houghton Mifflin Company, 1965), p. 111.

26. Erikson, *Insight and Responsibility*, pp. 49–80.

27. *Ibid.*, p. 72.

28. *Ibid.*, p. 72.

29. *Ibid.*, p. 75.

30. Martz, *The Poetry of Meditation*, p. 39.

31. Pruyser, *The Minister as Diagnostician*, pp. 95–96.

32. *Ibid.*, pp. 113–114.

33. Erikson, *Insight and Responsibility*, p. 53.

34. *Autobiography of Madame Guyon*, 2 vols., tr. by Thomas Taylor Allen (London: Kegan Paul, 1897). The following selection is from Vol. I. Some minor editing has been done.

35. Daniel Day Williams, *The Minister and the Care of Souls* (Harper & Brothers, 1961), p. 60.

36. Robert Jay Lifton, *The Life of the Self: Toward a New Psychology* (Simon & Schuster, Inc., 1976), pp. 32–33.

37. Robert Jay Lifton, *Death in Life: Survivors of Hiroshima* (Random House, Inc., 1967).

38. Robert Jay Lifton, "Protean Man," *Partisan Review*, Winter 1968, Vol. 35, No. 1.

39. *Ibid.*

40. Peter L. Berger, *A Rumor of Angels* (Doubleday & Company, Inc., Anchor Books, 1970), Ch. 3.

41. Barbara Herrnstein Smith, *Poetic Closure* (The University of Chicago Press, 1968), Ch. 3.

42. Evans and Parker, eds., *Christian Theology*, pp. 242–261. This case was written by Robert A. Evans and Alice Frazer Evans. (Headings have been supplied.) Used by permission of Robert A. Evans and Alice Frazer Evans.

43. The theologians, in the order cited, are Carl E. Braaten, Carl F. H. Henry, and Rosemary R. Ruether.

44. Evans and Parker, eds., *Christian Theology*, p. 245.

45. *Ibid.*, pp. 257–258.

46. Erikson, *Identity and the Life Cycle*, p. 98.

47. Robert Keaynes, "Proceedings of Excommunication Against Mistress Ann Hibbens of Boston (1640)," in John Demos, ed., *Remarkable Providences* (George Braziller, Inc., 1972), pp. 222–239.

48. Erikson, *Childhood and Society*, p. 252.

49. Demos, ed., *Remarkable Providences*, p. 227.

50. *Ibid.*, p. 235.

51. *Ibid.*, pp. 238–239.

52. John Demos, *A Little Commonwealth: Family Life in Plymouth Colony* (Oxford University Press, 1970), Ch. 9.

53. Aileen Ward, *John Keats: The Making of a Poet* (The Viking Press, Inc., 1963), pp. 297–299.

54. *Ibid.*

Gives pastoral care theory a solid foundation . . .

Much needed because it develops the thematic approach to the study of personality as a theoretical basis for pastoral care. This thematic approach, which includes the personality theories of Henry Murray, Robert W. White, Robert Jay Lifton, and especially Erik H. Erikson, is notable for its emphasis on personal and institutional change. The book emphasizes the role that pastoral care can play as a "change agent" in the local parish. Individual chapters discuss the thematic understanding of personality change, change in the local parish, pastoral counseling as a model for change, and the role of pastoral care in effecting change through personal and institutional crises. Selected case studies illustrate how the thematic approach applies to pastoral care situations. Primarily a contribution to pastoral psychology, it also touches on problems and issues in pastoral theology.

DONALD CAPPS is Associate Professor of Pastoral Care and Psychology of Religion, The Graduate Seminary, Phillips University. He also taught at the University of North Carolina at Charlotte and the University of Chicago Divinity School, where he received his Ph.D.

THE WESTMINSTER PRESS

ISBN 0-664-24222-7